MICKEY MANTLE

"Nobody knew how badly he was hurt."

The dream belonged to Elven (Mutt) Mantle. He carried it with him into the dark, dingy, depressing lead and zinc mines of Oklahoma. He lived with it through the ravages of the long struggles of the Depression. It fortified him through a life of toil and torment; a life of pain and privation. It was no more than any man wants for his son—to have a better life than he had—and Mutt Mantle was de-

termined to fight with all the strength he possessed to keep
his boy out of the mines, where illness and pain, frustration
and fear were a man's constant and inevitable companions.
Mutt Mantle knew the hardships of the mines, and he was
determined that his son would never know these things.

Mining was Mutt Mantle's life, but baseball was his
passion and his dream. Someday his son, yet unborn, would
be a big league baseball player. Someday his son would be
rich and famous, so rich and famous that he would never
have to go into the mines, that he would never have to face
a life in which you lived in constant fear of cave-ins and
mine sickness.

Mutt wanted his son to become a ballplayer. He even
had a name picked out for the boy. He would call him
Mickey after his favorite ballplayer, Mickey Cochrane, the
great Detroit Tiger catcher.

On October 20, 1931, in the tiny, dust-filled mining
town of Spavinaw, Oklahoma, Mutt Mantle's dream came
into the world. He was a robust little fellow, and the first
time Mutt Mantle saw him he knew that here was a son to
build a dream on.

At six months little Mickey had his first baseball cap,
knitted by his mother. At three he had his first baseball
uniform and, by the time he was five, he was learning to
be a switch-hitter. His dad would throw right-handed while
Mickey batted left, and his grandfather would throw left-
handed while Mickey batted right. Mutt Mantle was taking
no chances with his dream.

"I can't remember a time," Mickey says, "when I
wasn't wearing a glove, throwing a tennis ball against a
wall or hitting a tennis ball with a bat."

Mutt never discouraged his boy from playing any sport, and Mickey played them all—baseball, football, basketball—and while his dad had his dream, Mickey was doing a little dreaming of his own. He favored football, and he hoped someday to play for the University of Oklahoma.

At Commerce High School he was a halfback, not quite 165 pounds but fast and powerful. He had already begun to develop the thick neck, broad shoulders, strong wrists and forearms and powerful thighs that would, in later years, set him apart from most baseball players of his day. At the same time he began to develop another Mickey Mantle trademark—a susceptibility to injury.

In one game he was kicked in the left shin during a pileup, but shrugged it off and continued to play. The next day the leg was swollen and purple, and his father took him to a hospital in Oklahoma City where he underwent a long series of tests and X rays. Doctors discovered Mickey had a rare bone disease known as osteomyelitis, which could be arrested but not cured. It would leave the bones in a permanently weakened condition. For a time amputation was considered, but the doctors finally sent him home on crutches with orders to stay off the leg for six months. It was asking too much to expect a boy as active as Mickey to remain on crutches for that length of time. Besides, if he couldn't play for six months he would miss the entire high school baseball season. After two months he discarded the crutches and went out to play. From now on, he would stick to baseball.

During that period in the late 1940s, long before baseball's big bonuses, free-agent draft and complex, spylike scouting systems, teams still clung to the time-tested method of discovering talent. They employed scouts who operated like salesmen, going from door to door, following leads and hoping against hope to stumble upon a Bob Feller throwing rocks at a tin can on his father's farm in Iowa, or a Lou Gehrig smashing neighbors' windows with baseballs hit from a New York City sandlot.

Such a prospector was Tom Greenwade, a tall, slim, middle-aged gentleman with an uncanny eye for baseball talent. He prowled the Oklahoma area for the New York Yankees. One day, on his way to look at a shortstop in Broken Arrow, Oklahoma, Greenwade passed through Commerce, saw a baseball game in progress and stopped to take a look. He discovered Mickey Mantle playing shortstop for Commerce High.

On the day of his high school graduation, the Yankees signed Mantle for $1,500 in bonus and salary and sent him to their Class D farm club at Independence, Missouri, for the remainder of the season. The Yankees were looking for a young shortstop, someone to eventually replace Phil Rizzuto, and they were hoping Mantle might be their man.

By the end of Mickey's second season in organized ball, the Yankees were convinced of two things: they had in their possession a young man with the potential of becoming a truly great hitter, and they still needed a young shortstop to eventually replace Rizzuto. In his second year, playing for Joplin in the Class C Western Association, Mantle led the league in runs scored (141), hits (199), batting (.383) and errors (55). He also slugged 26 home runs, 12 triples, 30 doubles and knocked in 136 runs. The Yankees could hardly wait to see him in Phoenix, Arizona, their spring training base in 1951.

The great DiMaggio was at the end of his playing days in 1951. A bone spur on his heel had shortened his fabulous career. This was to be his last year, and the Yankees were searching desperately for a successor to Joe, their inspiring leader. When they looked at Mickey Mantle that spring and saw his explosive power from either side of the plate, his sudden burst of speed and his powerful throwing arm, the booming drives that propelled off the bat of this 20-year-old with a body chiseled out of concrete, they felt certain here was the star to continue the line of succession from Ruth to Gehrig to DiMaggio.

Casey Stengel, that wizened, gnarled old elf of prodigious memory and sharp eye, decided the boy must be moved to the outfield and brought to Yankee Stadium immediately. The front office protested, insisting the young man should first spend a year in Triple A ball, and perhaps they were right. For every gigantic, devastating home run he hit, there were five lusty, vicious strikeouts. On July 5 Stengel agreed it would be best to send the boy down to Kansas City.

Mickey was down all right. He was almost out. Disappointed and depressed, he failed to hit even in Kansas City. After twenty at bats he had just one hit, a bunt single. One day he had a surprise visitor—Mutt Mantle had come up from Commerce to take mournful inventory on a dream.

"How are things going?" he asked, sitting in Mickey's hotel room.

"Awful," Mickey replied. "I can't get a hit. The Yankees sent me down to learn not to strike out and now

I can't even get a hit. I'm not good enough to play in the major leagues and I'm not good enough to play here. I'll never make it. I think I'll quit and go home with you."

"Well, Mick," his father said quietly, "if that's all the guts you have I think you'd better quit. You might as well come home right now."

Mutt Mantle never had much formal education, but he must have learned a great deal about psychology down in the mines. Instead of sympathy he offered resignation and acceptance. Instead of a pep talk there was seeming disinterest. If his father had insisted, begged, pleaded, ordered, Mickey would have stayed and resented it and felt chained to baseball. Instead, Mutt Mantle did not insist, did not beg, did not plead, did not order, and because of this the younger Mantle was free to choose. He knew how much his father wanted him to stay. He knew how disappointed his father would be if he went home to the mines, and Mickey did not want to hurt his father. He was free to go home or to stay . . . and he stayed.

Mickey got 59 hits in his next 146 at bats, hit 13 home runs and drove in 50 runs. Soon he was back in Yankee Stadium, and Mutt Mantle was sitting in the stands, watching his boy playing in the World Series against the New York Giants.

It was the second game of the 1951 Series. Willie Mays hit a high, lazy pop to right center and Mutt watched his boy running after it. Suddenly he saw him fall to the ground, writhing in pain. They carried Mickey off the field on a stretcher. He had stepped on a drainage spout, seriously injuring his right knee. He went to the hospital in a

United Press International Photo

*Mickey crumples at DiMaggio's feet in the 1951 series. This was
the first of Mantle's long string of injuries.*

taxi and his dad went with him. When they arrived Mutt got
out first and Mickey climbed out after him, placing his
hand on his dad's shoulder for support. As he did, Mutt
buckled and collapsed on the sidewalk. They told Mickey
his dad was very sick with Hodgkin's disease, a cancer of

the blood. After Mickey's knee operation he took his dad to the Mayo Clinic in Rochester, Minnesota, for treatments. It was the last time Mickey saw his father alive. Mutt Mantle died a few months later, but he died a happy man. He had seen his dream come true.

The great DiMaggio was out of the Yankee organization in 1952, and in his place in center field was the young slugger, Mickey Mantle. A new era was beginning in the illustrious history of the New York Yankees.

For the next ten years Mickey Mantle would be the dominant figure in baseball. He was exciting. He was explosive. He was awesome. He exuded strength and raw power. His prodigious wallops carried to distant places never before reached by man. In 1953 he powered a ball over the left field bleachers in Washington's Griffith Stadium that was measured at 565 feet, giving rise to a new expression in the language of baseball—the tape measure home run. It soon became standard practice to have Mantle's home runs surveyed, their distances recorded. Like the one he hit in Chicago's Comiskey Park: 550 feet. During an exhibition game he became the third player to hit a ball over the right field roof in Pittsburgh. In 1956 he almost became the first man to hit a fair ball out of Yankee Stadium; the drive crashed against the facade on top of the third deck in right field. He was the first man to reach the center field bleachers in Yankee Stadium, the first to drive a ball over the center field wall in Pittsburgh, the second to hit one over the right field wall in Kansas City.

He kept American League teams in the black. Fans by the thousands came to see him play in Cleveland, De-

troit, Boston, Washington. They came to see him hit one
of his big home runs, and he rarely disappointed them.
Everything he did was big. The way he ran, the way he
threw, the way he swung. Even his strikeouts frightened
you, while they tortured him.

Mickey was a difficult man in his early days. He was
sullen and brooding. When he struck out he was booed, and
he would throw his cap, toss his bat skyward, kick water
coolers, slam his fist into walls. The more he raved, the
more he was booed. It was not that they disliked Mickey.
Rather, it seemed they were trying to goad him into reach-
ing the moon. They had seen him hit those powerful drives
and, having seen them, they would accept nothing less. The
newspapers told them nothing was beyond his reach, and
when he did anything short of perfection they were disappointed. So they booed. And Mantle raved.

He was not bitter toward them. He was not reacting to
the boos, but was chastising himself. Failure tormented him.

"Mickey has fierce pride," said his friend, Whitey
Ford, who understood him. "When he's really discouraged,
it's because he feels he has let the team down. He feels he's
got to be the best because everybody expects him to be the
best, everybody depends on him so much."

His teammates depended on him, but the press attacked him. They said he was squandering his vast talents
with his temperamental outbursts. They said he was a
spoiled child, that he did not have the desire to excel that
the great DiMaggio had. It puzzled Mickey. "Why," he
asked, "do they think I throw my helmet and kick water
coolers?"

He was the driving force of a Yankee dynasty that won eight pennants and six world championships in those ten years. It seemed that anything he wanted to do he could do. When he wanted to hit home runs, he hit 54 in 1961. When he wanted to drive in runs, he knocked in 130 in 1956. When he wanted to hit for a high average, he batted .365 in 1957. When he wanted to steal bases, he stole 21 in 1959. And when he wanted to put it all together, he won the triple crown in 1956 with 52 home runs, 130 RBI's and a .353 batting average, and walked off with the first of his three Most Valuable Player trophies.

But, through it all, he was plagued with a succession of minor injuries that chipped away, but could not destroy, the monument of achievements he would leave to baseball. He had torn ligaments and pulled muscles, shin splints, bruises and minor fractures. He played with pain and with minor hurts.

Then it was 1961, and what could have been his greatest year turned into his saddest. Late in the season he developed an injury that was to be the beginning of a series of misfortunes which would reduce him from a man of incredible animal strength to an almost helpless cripple.

It was the year of the home run, Mickey Mantle and Roger Maris matching one another shot for shot in the greatest, most captivating home run race in baseball history. Into September they roared, each with a chance to break Babe Ruth's fabled record of sixty home runs in a single season, a record which had withstood the challenge of the game's great sluggers for 34 years. Maris set the pace right from the start, and Mantle chased him. On

September 2 Maris hit his 52nd and 53rd to go five up on
Mantle, but the following day Mickey hit his 49th and
50th. On September 9 Maris hit number 56, and the next
day Mantle hit number 53. With seventeen games left they
were both still in the race against Ruth, but Mickey had
been playing with a virus and, on September 18, he suc-
cumbed to the bug and to the Babe and checked into a
hospital for treatment. He returned on September 23 to
hit his 54th homer. It was his last game of the season. An
immediate relapse put him back into the hospital. Maris
went on to hit his 61st home run while Mantle recuperated
in a hospital.

The Yankees won the pennant and prepared to meet
the Cincinnati Reds, champions of the National League,
without their leader, Mantle. But this was one World Series
Mickey refused to miss. He dragged himself out of the
hospital bed and declared himself ready to play.

Manager Ralph Houk refused to use him in the first
two games in New York. The Yankees won the first and
the Reds won the second. The two teams moved to Crosley
Field, Cincinnati. Sensing a struggle, Houk called on his
injured star for game number three. Mickey, still suffering
from an open abscess on his hip which had developed during his hospital stay, wrapped his wound with pads of
gauze and went out to play.

Pain was reflected in his face every time he put pressure on his leg, but the Yankees won the third game, 3–2,
and Mantle was in the lineup for game number four, winc-
ing with pain whenever he was forced to come down hard
on his left leg.

In the fourth inning he lined a smash to left field and hobbled to first. His uniform was red where the blood from the open wound had soaked through the gauze onto his pants' leg, and Houk removed him for a pinch runner. When the game was over and the Yankees had won, 7–0, players came into the dressing room but did not go directly to their lockers. One by one they went into the trainer's room, where Mantle lay on a table having the wound treated. They went to him silently to shake his hand in a way that told him of their gratitude.

"It made me sick to look at the hole in his hip," said Elston Howard. "It makes me sick to think about it. Nobody else would have played. Nobody. But Mickey isn't like normal people."

Said manager Houk: "Nobody knew how badly he was hurt. He never sat near me, so I didn't know what was happening. When I took him out of the game his face was white. Most guys would have been in bed, but he was trying to stretch singles into doubles."

Mantle came back full throttle in 1962. He hit the ball well in spring training and in the early part of the season. You could tell it was going to be another great year. You could tell it until the night of May 18 in Yankee Stadium.

The Yankees were playing the Minnesota Twins, and they came into the bottom of the ninth inning with the Twins leading 4–3 and Mantle batting with two out and nobody on, trying to get on base. He swung and smashed the ball with a power and force that few men can generate. If he had gotten under the ball just a little, he would have hit it out of sight, but he hit on top of it and drove it on one hop between short and third. Out of nowhere came Zoilo Versalles, the scrappy little shortstop of the Twins, to backhand the ball, straighten up and throw. . . . It was going to be close at first. Mantle, realizing he had to get on base to keep the game going, was pounding down the line with a burst of speed in that awkward, flat-footed way he runs, head down, knees churning like pistons. Then, ten feet from the bag, he toppled over like a felled deer, writhing on the ground, digging his fingernails into the dirt in agonizing pain.

"It felt like somebody took a knife and stuck it in there," Mantle said. "The leg was up in the air and it wouldn't go down. I was hurt bad. I said to myself, 'You hurt yourself again.' That was all I could think . . . *again*."

They said he would be out a week—he was out five with a pulled groin muscle. It was too bad, because it might have been his greatest year. He batted .321, hit 30 home runs and knocked in 89 runs in only 377 at bats. He was the league's Most Valuable Player, and he showed why on the afternoon of June 16 in Cleveland. He had not batted in five weeks, but the Yankees trailed, 7–6, with two on in the eighth. Houk looked at Mantle, and Mickey grabbed a bat and went up to the plate to pinch-hit. Not a word was said between the man and the manager.

He swung. A drive rocketed into the right field seats for a home run. The Indians were leading the league at the time, and there were 70,000 fans in Municipal Stadium that day filled with the anticipation of victory. They watched Mantle crush their hopes and they rose, in spite of their disappointment, and gave him a standing ovation. In the

Yankee dugout they were standing too, aware that they had just witnessed one of the most courageous acts ever performed on a ballfield.

It was almost the same thing all over again in 1963. Another great spring, another fast start, and then a cool June 5 night in Baltimore. A long drive to center off the bat of Brooks Robinson sent Mantle back to the wire fence . . . then a sickening crash and, for a brief instant, Mantle draped on the fence like a prisoner gunned down while trying to scale the prison wall. He toppled heavily to the ground and was removed from the outfield on a stretcher. He was taken by ambulance to a hospital to have his broken foot put in a cast. Returning when the game was over, Mantle sat in front of his locker, his left leg in a cast, a look of frustration on his face. "Every time I'm going good," he said, "something happens. It's got to happen, I guess. Sooner or later, it's got to happen." He picked up his left shoe. "I won't be needing this for a while."

He reached for his crutches and got up to leave. "Do you know how to use those things?" somebody asked.

"I've lived with them," he replied, sadly.

Mantle missed a month. When he came back it was still no good. While his foot was being treated his left knee was ignored, and the forced inactivity weakened it to such an extent that he was of little use that year. It was a season wasted, and without their great leader the Yankees floundered and struggled, weakened by his absence which only emphasized their appreciation of his talents.

"He's our inspiration," Bobby Richardson said, "and he doesn't realize it. I just wish he were healthy."

Added Jim Bouton: "Even when he's not playing it's his voice you hear cheering you on from the dugout. He wants to win so badly that to match his desire you want to put out just as much yourself. You want to go out and win for him."

And Elston Howard said: "We need him. We do better when he's just sitting around."

The Yankees needed him in 1963, and he came back late in the season. He played in only 65 games, but he batted .314 and hit 15 home runs and he was there, just sitting around, and they won the pennant.

When he played it was with a fury and a strange fatalism, going all out in a way that seemed to say, "If this is going to be my last game, let it be a good one." His teammates and friends cautioned him to go slowly, to save himself, to protect his fragile body. There were days when he should have rested, but he played. "If you start sitting out," he reasoned, "the first thing you know you're sitting them all out. It gets easier and easier to do it, and I don't want to be a guy who just sits around."

So he shrugged off the pain and played, and he also shrugged off the thought that he was doing something heroic. "The only thing I can do is play baseball," he said. "I have to play ball. It's the only thing I know. So it doesn't matter if my legs hurt, I've got to play. What else would I do?"

He had one big, all-out pop left in that deteriorating body and he shot it in 1964. It was a year free of serious injury. There were only minor ones, and he had stopped counting those a long time ago. He felt good, he told a reporter. "Nothing hurts me except my legs," he said. "But they always hurt." He missed only 19 games. It was considered a triumph. He batted .303, had 35 home runs and drove in 111 runs. Once again he led the Yankees into the World Series and led himself into his most satisfying moment.

It came on Saturday, October 10, in the third game of the World Series. The Cardinals had won the first game and the Yankees the second, and they came into the bottom of the ninth of the third game with the score tied, 1–1. Mantle was the first batter when Barney Schultz, veteran knuckle ball pitcher, came out of the bullpen to throw nine knuckle balls, eight of them warming up.

Mantle sent the ninth one soaring high and far into the right field seats. It was his sixteenth World Series home run, breaking Babe Ruth's record, and it won the game. As he loped around the bases in that regal trot, Yankees came pouring out of the dugout to pound his back and to shake his hand. "It gives me a bigger thrill than anything," he said, "to please my own teammates. It makes you feel good to make them happy."

Mickey Mantle has made them happy thousands of times. Just being there has made them happy, even in 1965 when it all came apart for him. He was a part-time player then, and the Yankees sank to sixth place, their lowest standing in forty years. Mickey Mantle was coming to the end, and there was nobody coming along to take his place as he had taken the place of Joe DiMaggio, DiMaggio of Lou Gehrig and Gehrig of Babe Ruth. The line of great succession was ending.

His shoulder hurt from an injury he suffered in the 1957 World Series against the Milwaukee Braves. He couldn't throw and he could hardly run. He was being betrayed by his own magnificent body. He was being sabotaged by his powerful muscles, which had broken down, eroding his matchless skills. Johnny Keane was his manager then, the fourth one to be touched by the courage of this remarkable man. "I don't want him taking chances on those legs of his. But telling him not to run is like talking to that wall over there. You can't imagine what it means just to have him in there, playing half-mast as he has been."

The measure of Mickey Mantle is not in the base hits he has made or the prodigious home runs he has hit or the great records he has set. The measure of Mickey Mantle is in the admiration and the respect he gets from his colleagues.

It is in the words of Early Wynn: "I played with him in an all-star game and I watched him dress. I watched him bandage that knee—that whole leg—and I saw what he had to go through in order to play, and now I'll never be able to say enough in praise of him. Seeing those legs, his power becomes unbelievable."

It is in the words of Billy Martin: "I know what a great price he's paid to be the best. There were a lot of times he played when the average guy would have sat out. That's why he's the best there is."

It is in the words of Clete Boyer: "You can't describe him. You have to watch him day after day, the taping, the pain, the tremendous force he plays the game with. He's the man we would all like to be."

It is in the words of Carl Yastrzemski: "I see him swing sometimes, and even from the outfield you can see the leg buckle under him and the way he winces in pain. I wince, too. It's like your own kid is in pain and you can feel the pain yourself. That's the way ballplayers feel about Mantle."

And, of course, it is in the words of Casey Stengel: "He's the only man I ever saw who was a cripple and could outdo the world."

He would go on to hit over 500 home runs and play in more games than any other Yankee and yet, when they would talk about him or write about him they would say what a pity that he did not have a healthy body because he would have been the greatest; he would have outdone them all. After sixteen years in the major leagues he had played in 2,113 games—he was only a pinch hitter in almost 100 of them, and he was at less than top physical shape in more than 1,000. He had missed 341 games completely—more than two full seasons—and there is no saying what records he might have put into the books. But Mickey Mantle has never asked for sympathy. He has no regrets. "It hasn't been very hard for me," he says. "I've been lucky. I feel like I have been very lucky to play for the Yankees."

He is not an emotional man, yet he was moved by what happened on September 18, 1965. It was Mickey Mantle Day in Yankee Stadium, and he stood at home plate surrounded by his family, friends and teammates while 60,000 worshippers showered him with love and affection from the stands. He thought about his dad and how proud he would have been. He looked up at the big old ballpark packed with fans right up to the third tier and he was moved.

They cheered for him and told of their appreciation for the times he thrilled them with his hitting and for the times he played when he was hurt. They told him with their applause and with their cheers and they told him with the signs that sprinkled the stands. WE LOVE MICKEY, said one. MICKEY IS THE GREATEST, said another. The papers had reported that he might not come back in 1966 and the fans wanted him back, for if he quit it would be the end of something great, of something to hang on to. And because of this there was another sign: DON'T QUIT MICKEY.

Mickey Mantle quit? He never learned the meaning of the word.

JOHNNY UNITAS

"I'm sorry, but we can't use you. We're letting you go."

Darkness was falling on the sleepy little upstate New York town of Olean. The night air coming down from the mountains had brought a brief relief from the oppressive August heat. There was a stillness about the town and traffic moved slowly on Highway 17, where a crewcut young man, suitcase in hand, stood waiting, hoping some considerate motorist would pick him up.

The last bus had left Olean for Pittsburgh hours ago, but the young man could not wait for morning. He could not stay another minute in that town. He would hitchhike the 160 miles to his home.

He was leaving the football training camp of the Pittsburgh Steelers, where less than an hour ago a dream had died slowly and painfully. It had died when coach Walt Kiesling called him into his office and clubbed him over the head with about as much subtlety as a punch on the jaw. "I'm sorry," Kiesling had said, "but we can't use you. We're letting you go. We've got three quarterbacks ahead of you."

The words cut into him like a knife. He had come so close. In a week the team would be breaking camp and the young quarterback had felt certain he would be with them when they did. He was hurt and puzzled because the man picked ahead of him as third-string quarterback was Vic Eaton, another rookie who had been picked two rounds behind him in the college draft. The young quarterback had worked hard and waited for a chance that never came. He had clung to a dream that would never be realized, and with all the waiting there was frustration and bitterness and despair.

None of it made sense, but what could he do? Would it help to complain to coach Kiesling that he had not been given a fair chance to make the team? Would it help to tell him how much he wanted to play professional football; how he had dreamed about it ever since he was a kid? Would it help to tell him that he had a wife back home in Pittsburgh and a child and another one on the way and that he was broke, so broke he had to live with his in-laws?

As he waited on Highway 17 he thought how tough it was going to be to tell Dotty. They had both counted so much on him making the team. It was not a big contract, just $6,000, but it was a start and to them it seemed a fortune. Now here he was, on his way back to Pittsburgh to face Dotty and the baby, with nothing to show for all those months of preparation and hard work except $10 the Steelers had given him for bus fare. It was the disappointment and frustration that disturbed him, not the hard work and rejection. He had known hard work and rejection all his life and he feared neither.

When Johnny Unitas was five his father, who operated a coal-delivery truck, passed away, leaving his mother with four young children to feed and clothe and care for. Those were difficult days, and Johnny grew up in hard times. Money was scarce, and his mother worked very hard to provide for her children. She kept up her husband's business. She took orders and drove the truck herself while Johnny and his older brother, Len, loaded and unloaded the truck.

Johnny's mother could not give him the guidance and companionship that only a father can give a growing boy, but she taught her son something very fine and very valuable. She taught him courage and perseverance. "She never got discouraged and she taught us kids to think the same way," Johnny recalls. "Mother never liked football because she was afraid I'd get hurt. Yet by explaining what it takes to get ahead, she taught me more about football than any of my coaches . . . and I've played for some very good ones."

Football and John Unitas found each other at Pittsburgh's St. Justin's High School. He made the school team as a freshman and was a starting halfback his first two years. In his junior year Johnny was shifted to end, but when the quarterback broke his ankle, coach Jim Carey picked Unitas as the emergency replacement because he had the strongest throwing arm on the team. It turned out to be a fortunate decision . . . both for St. Justin's and Johnny Unitas.

In less than two seasons Unitas threw 22 touchdown passes. Although he did not play on a championship team, he was named to the Pittsburgh All-Catholic team in both his junior and senior year. Johnny was motivated by just one thing—to play professional football—and as preparation he planned to enroll in the best and most prestigious football college that would accept him. He aimed for the very top. With help from several alumni in the Pittsburgh area, a tryout was arranged for him at Notre Dame.

He spent a week under the Golden Dome and under the eye of backfield coach Bernie Crimmins. Crimmins liked the way Johnny handled himself and he liked the way he threw the football, but he didn't like the way he was built. Reluctantly, he told Unitas Notre Dame could not use him.

"I'm afraid you'll never be big enough to play college football," Crimmins said, and Johnny, a strapping six-footer but a skinny 145 pounds, could not dispute the point.

He was disappointed but not discouraged. He went to the University of Indiana for another tryout. He threw the ball better than ever, and he felt sure he impressed the coaches because when he left they said they would contact him. He never heard another word. Not a yes, not a no, not a maybe. Nothing.

Back home, Johnny was contacted by Len Casanova, head coach at the University of Pittsburgh. He had seen Johnny play at St. Justin's, had read about him and heard about him from several high school coaches. There was a scholarship waiting for John at Pitt if he wanted it. There would be no tryouts, just a routine entrance examination. The idea of playing in his home town appealed to Johnny. And Pittsburgh played a big-time schedule, so he was certain to get the proper attention from pro scouts if he did well. But, although he had been a better than average student at St. Justin's, Johnny failed the entrance examination.

Unitas was crushed. The fall semester was about to begin and John's chances of getting into a college grew slim. But St. Justin coach Carey recalled a chance meeting at a football clinic with John Dromo, assistant coach at the University of Louisville, who expressed a desire to land a boy who could throw the football. Carey never mentioned Unitas, knowing Johnny had his heart set on a big school. In desperation Carey called Dromo, who contacted Unitas immediately.

At first John declined with thanks. He preferred to wait a year and try to get into a bigger school. But Dromo persisted. He pointed out that he had coached George Ratterman in high school and Ratterman had been an outstanding schoolboy passer; he had gone on to Notre Dame to sit on the bench watching Johnny Lujack play quarterback. At Louisville Unitas would get a chance to play. He would not be lost in the shuffle of sixty or seventy high school All-Americans battling for a handful of jobs.

Unitas was convinced, and at Louisville he discovered that Dromo had not exaggerated. Coach Frank Camp had a

weak team, and because Louisville was not a member of
the NCAA, Johnny was permitted to play as a freshman to
fill out the varsity squad. So as an eighteen-year-old kid
just out of St. Justin's High, Johnny Unitas was the third-
string quarterback for the University of Louisville, which
played an ambitious schedule with such teams as North
Carolina State, Houston, Cincinnati, Mississippi Southern.

The team lost three of its first four games. In the fifth
game, against St. Bonaventure, Louisville fell behind, 19–0.
At halftime coach Camp decided it was time to do something drastic. He could think of nothing more drastic than
to put the skinny kid in at quarterback and let him throw
until he got tired. Johnny did not muff his chance. He completed eleven straight passes and pushed Louisville into a
21–19 lead. A late field goal gave St. Bonaventure a 22–21
victory, but it was a profitable defeat for coach Camp. He
lost a game, but he found a quarterback.

Playing a freshman at quarterback was a big gamble,
but Camp figured he had little to lose. He planned to keep
Unitas as his number one quarterback for the remainder
of the season, which consisted of games against North Carolina State, Houston, Washington and Lee and Mississippi
Southern. If nothing else, Louisville would be building for
the future. Not even coach Camp could have hoped for
what happened in those four remaining games. Louisville,
with its young quarterback throwing eight touchdown
passes, won all four to finish with a respectable 5–4 record.

He was only eighteen and he didn't look like much,
but Johnny Unitas could throw the football, and he had
remarkable poise for one so young. It was an indescribable,

intangible something that was infectious. He aroused a team. He imbued it with spirit and confidence. He was a winner.

In Johnny's sophomore year Louisville won only three of eight games. The five defeats were not an indictment of Unitas. Rather, the three victories were a miracle considering the quality of the rest of the team. He completed 50 percent of his passes and threw for twelve touchdowns. He was Louisville's only offensive threat. Opposing coaches praised him, newspapermen raved over him and Louisville students idolized him.

Unitas was Mr. Big on campus, but on the rare occasions when he could put together enough money to go home to Pittsburgh—on a milk train that made so many stops it took seventeen hours to make the trip—he realized something was missing. He might be a hero in Louisville, but he was practically unknown in his home town. He longed for recognition and attention he would get at a bigger school.

When John returned for his junior year, he discovered that misfortune had struck the school: fifteen of the team's football players had been suspended for academic deficiency, leaving the squad with just a handful of experienced players. The next two years would be disastrous.

Just then, Unitas was contacted by Bernie Crimmins, the man who had turned him down at Notre Dame. Crimmins had become head coach at Indiana University and had been reading about Unitas. He desperately needed a quarterback, and he had checked with the authorities and determined that Unitas could transfer to Indiana without any loss of eligibility simply by sitting out a year. Unitas knew it would be a great opportunity for him to play in the tough, well-publicized, well-scouted Big Ten conference. Players from Indiana made it big in the pros every year, but how many players from Louisville had ever played pro ball?

The offer was very tempting. Johnny consulted his mother and his high school coach, Jim Carey, for their advice. His mother was not sure, although her basic instincts told her there was something wrong about leaving a school where he had been welcomed and idolized. Coach Carey was more emphatic. "When you needed this guy Crimmins," he said, "he didn't want you. Now that he wants you, he's asking you to give up a year of your life. It's a very important decision, but you'll have to make it yourself. I can't help you."

John Unitas made the decision himself. He decided to stay at Louisville, and he wondered if it was a decision he would live to regret. Louisville won only four games in Unitas' last two seasons. He was the team's entire offense, and he even played the last year with a hairline fracture of the ankle. When he was drafted ninth by the Pittsburgh Steelers, he was confident everything had worked out for the best.

But now, eight months later, walking down a Pittsburgh street, tired from hitching rides and traveling all night, discouraged by failure, he was not sure.

John Unitas was down, but he was not out. He still had some fight left in him; he still had some hope and he still had a great deal of confidence. The first thing he did when he arrived home was send a telegram to Paul Brown of the Cleveland Browns asking for a tryout. The Browns had scouted him at Louisville, and the scout told Johnny they

were planning to draft him on about the twelfth round if
he was still available. He was not.

The following day Johnny received an answer from
Brown. He thanked Unitas for getting in touch with him, but
he said the Browns were set at quarterback for that season
because Otto Graham had decided to postpone his retirement and would play one more year. However, there was
a good chance they would be looking for a quarterback next
year, and Brown invited Unitas to check with him again.

That was the one bit of hope Johnny needed. That was
the encouragement and incentive he needed to keep himself
in shape for one more chance. One more chance, that was
all he wanted. He knew he would make it if he got just one
more chance.

The year that followed was the most difficult Johnny
ever experienced. It was a year of hard work, struggle and
counting pennies to make ends meet. Only the thought of
another chance in professional football kept him going. He
could have had a job as a high school physical education
teacher but that would have been quitting, and Johnny
Unitas was not a quitter. Instead, he took the kind of job
that would keep him fit and hard for his shot with the
Browns—working as a piledriver on a construction gang.

Soon after his return to Pittsburgh, a former Louisville teammate asked him if he would be interested in playing football for a semipro team in suburban Pittsburgh, the
Bloomfield Rams. They needed a quarterback and they were
willing to pay Johnny $6 a game. He grabbed the chance.
It was an immeasurable distance from the Bloomfield Rams
to the NFL, and many times Johnny regretted his decision
to join the Rams, who played on distant fields littered with

glass and rocks. He regretted the time lost and the humiliation, but the money came in handy. Besides, playing every
week helped him sharpen his passing.

When Johnny's big chance finally arrived, it was not
from the Cleveland Browns. It came from the Baltimore
Colts. It came in the form of a telephone call one night
from Baltimore general manager Don Kellett, who said the
Colts were looking for a number two quarterback behind
George Shaw to replace Gary Kerkorian, who had decided
to quit the game to study for a law degree. If Johnny was
interested, Kellett continued, he could come to Baltimore
in May and work out for coach Weeb Ewbank. If Ewbank
liked him, Unitas would be invited to the Colts' summer
training camp, with a chance to make the team for a starting
salary of $7,000. Johnny said a silent word of thanks for
Gary Kerkorian and the blessings of higher education, and
answered a loud "yes" to everything Kellett said.

Kellett was pleased at his success with Unitas. Good
quarterbacks, even unknown ones, were tough to come by
in those days, and the Colts' total investment in Unitas was
80¢, the cost of a telephone call from Baltimore to Pittsburgh. It was to be the greatest bargain in the history of
professional football.

There are several conflicting stories on just how the
Colts learned of Unitas, but Ewbank says it came about
through an anonymous letter about a sensational passer
who was playing sandlot ball in the Pittsburgh area. "I
always accused Johnny of writing that letter himself," Ewbank says kiddingly.

The name Unitas was familiar to Ewbank. Weeb was
an old friend and former college opponent of Frank Camp,

Johnny's college coach, and Ewbank remembered Camp mentioning the boy to him when Unitas was a senior. Ewbank went back into the Colts' files for the scouting report on Unitas and, sure enough, the Colts had rated him highly. They had had him on their draft list, but not high because they were well supplied with quarterbacks at the time. They planned to draft him if they got the chance, but the Steelers beat them to it.

Still, one thing disturbed Ewbank. To ease his mind, he put in a call to Louisville to see if Frank Camp could shed any light on why Unitas failed to make the Pittsburgh club. "John wrote me a letter shortly after he came home," Camp said. "He said he didn't feel the Steelers gave him much of an opportunity to make the team. He has an idea they found out he once failed the entrance examination at the University of Pittsburgh and figured he was not intelligent enough to run a pro team." By a strange coincidence, Ewbank had just signed a new line coach, Herman Ball, who had come from Pittsburgh and was in the Steelers' camp at Olean when Unitas was there. Ewbank checked with Ball, who upheld Unitas' story completely. The boy never had a chance, Ball agreed.

Professional football's intricate and mysterious spy network was working overtime in the case of Johnny Unitas, and because of it, Ewbank asked Kellett to contact Unitas and invite him to try out with the Colts.

This time Johnny did not fail. He impressed Ewbank enough in Baltimore to earn an invitation to training camp, and he impressed Ewbank so much in training camp that he made the team as the number two quarterback behind George Shaw. There seemed little chance Johnny would get to play very much, but he had a pro uniform and a job and, most important, he had a contract for $7,000 a year, $1,000 more than the Steelers were going to pay him.

The truly significant events in sports are often overlooked in their time. Frequently, they happen quite unobtrusively and with little fanfare. For instance, on June 2, 1925, Miller Huggins, diminutive manager of the New York Yankees, marched up to a strapping, powerful young man in the Yankee clubhouse and barked, "Pipp has a headache. You play first base today." Thus Lou Gehrig replaced the veteran Wally Pipp at first base and went on to play in 2,130 consecutive games as a Yankee, becoming one of the greatest players in baseball history.

On October 21, 1956, the Baltimore Colts were in Chicago, playing the Bears in the fourth game of the season. The Colts had lost two of their first three games. They were leading the Bears 20–14 in the third period when three monstrous Bear linemen piled on George Shaw, breaking his left leg. The next thing Johnny Unitas knew, he was crouched behind the Colts' center, calling signals.

It would be nice to say Unitas led Baltimore to a smashing victory over the Bears and a great star was born. It would be nice, but it would not be true.

The first pass Unitas threw was intercepted by J. C. Caroline and run back for a touchdown. On the first play after the kickoff, Unitas juggled a handoff, fumbled, and Chicago recovered and went on to score another touchdown. Another missed handoff, another fumble, another Chicago recovery and touchdown, and the Colts were out of the game. The Bears won, 58–27.

It had been a pitiful debut, but Unitas was not dis-

couraged. He knew he would get another chance the following week because the Colts had no other quarterback. And,
to help him forget, coach Ewbank completely absolved
Unitas of any blame for the bad beating. "The boy wasn't
ready mentally," Ewbank pointed out. "He didn't expect to
play and he had to come off the bench ice cold. He hadn't
worked out with the first string backfield often enough for
them to know his moves and him to know theirs. I still think
he's going to help us."

Ewbank is a gentle and patient man. He has the portly
build and demeanor that reminds you of a beardless Santa
Claus. He had been under fire from the Baltimore fans,
among the most fiercely loyal and outspoken in all of sports,
and his job was in serious jeopardy. It was therefore a kind
and courageous thing he did taking Unitas off the hook.
Unitas would be the starting quarterback against the Green
Bay Packers the following week.

It was a tremendous lift for Johnny, and he did not
squander the opportunity. He directed the team to a 28–21
victory, completing eight of sixteen passes for 100 yards
and two touchdowns. The following week it was the Cleveland Browns, defending champions of the world and a team
the Colts had never beaten. The Colts scored a smashing
21–7 upset and, although Johnny completed only five of
fourteen passes, the statistics did not reflect his true value to
the victory; they did not take into account his brilliant play-
calling. The following week against the Detroit Lions,
Unitas gained 324 yards passing, but all the breaks went
against the Colts and they were beaten, 27–3. The Colts lost
the game, but Unitas lost none of the luster he had been
rapidly accumulating week by week. The Colts were two-

for-three with Unitas at the controls and that, after all, is the quarterback's job: to win.

Unitas had the confidence now. He had won the first-string job and he would never relinquish it, even after Shaw had fully recovered from his broken leg.

Next came the Los Angeles Rams, and Unitas put on a show which surpassed any performance ever seen in Baltimore's Memorial Stadium. He completed 18 of 24 passes for 293 yards and three touchdowns as the Colts swamped the Rams, 56–21. It was the best single performance by any quarterback in the NFL that year.

The Colts were by no means a team of championship caliber in 1956, but the passing of their sensational, unknown rookie quarterback kept them in every game for the remainder of the season. They lost their next three, but finished the season with a stunning 19–17 victory over their archrivals and neighbors, the Washington Redskins. It was a 53-yard touchdown pass by Unitas with fifteen seconds remaining that pulled out the victory.

After a horrendous start, the Colts had finished with a five and seven record for fourth place in the Western Division. They had split their last eight games, thus saving coach Ewbank's job, exciting the Baltimore fans about the prospects for 1957 and establishing Johnny Unitas as the team's number one quarterback. He had completed 55.6 percent of his passes, a league record for a rookie.

The months following the 1956 season were considerably more pleasant and carefree for the Unitas family than the previous year. There was no more piledriving or playing semipro football on a rockpile for $6 a game. Mostly Johnny took it easy during the off-season and eagerly looked forward to going to camp the following summer as the number one Colts' quarterback with a new contract calling for a healthy raise.

But one season does not make a star, and Unitas still had to prove himself in 1957. He had to prove 1956 was no mistake. He had to triumph over the much-talked about, much-exaggerated sophomore jinx.

When the 1957 season ended, Johnny left little doubt he was the real thing. He completed 172 passes out of 301 attempts for 2,550 yards and 24 touchdowns, four short of the league record set by the great Sid Luckman against wartime competition in 1943. Johnny suffered three broken ribs and a collapsed lung in a game against the Green Bay Packers, but he did not miss a game. The next week he was back—wearing an aluminum corset insulated with sponge rubber to protect his ribs.

For most of the year Unitas had the Colts in contention for the Western Division championship, but they lost their last two games to finish in third place with a record of seven and five. It was the first time in the team's six-year history that they had finished over .500, and the rabid Baltimore fans looked ahead to 1958 with only one thing in mind. Championship!

They had been waiting a long time, but their dream finally came true. The Colts won their first six games in 1958, lost a tough one to the New York Giants, 24–21, then won their next three to breeze to the Western Division title. When they faced the Giants again on December 28, 1958, they were playing for the championship of all of professional football.

There have been many great moments in the career of

John Constantine Unitas. A list of his records would fill this page. He has already thrown more touchdown passes than any other player and, when he finally retires, he will also have attempted and completed more passes for more yardage than anyone else in the history of the game. He has a fantastic string of throwing touchdown passes in 47 consecutive games from 1956 to 1960, a record so incredible it probably will never be equalled. He ranks with Baugh, Luckman, Graham, Tittle and Layne among the all-time great quarterbacks, and most people think his name belongs on top of that list.

But what fans will remember above all else, what thrust him into the full focus of public attention and acclaim, what established him as a giant among giants, happened in New York's Yankee Stadium on that bitterly cold, clear Sunday, December 28, 1958. It has been called "the greatest football game ever played." Certainly, it was draped with all the excitement and all the drama that makes the game great. . . . There were the Giants, fiercely proud of their most stubborn of defenses. . . . There were the Colts, brimming with offensive power and led by a daring quarterback who laughed in the face of tradition and conservatism. . . . And there were 64,185 fans, whose wild enthusiasm rocked the stately old Stadium.

The Giants scored first on a 36-yard field goal by Pat Summerall. But the Colts came back to score two touchdowns in the second period, the second on a 15-yard pass from Unitas to Raymond Berry. The Colts left the field at halftime with a 14–3 lead.

In the second half the Giant defense went to work in

earnest. The Colts had a first down on the Giant three, but this stubborn and proud defense stopped the drive, took the ball away and turned the game around. The Giants marched for a touchdown to make it 14–10. Then the Giant defense stopped the Colts again, took the ball away and the Giants scored another touchdown to lead 17–14.

There were just two minutes remaining when the Colts got the ball on their own 14. Two minutes to move 86 yards —or to surrender their dream and start all over again next year. There were no time-outs left and no time for huddles. There was time only for throwing passes and Johnny Unitas threw them . . . seven in succession. He completed three to Raymond Berry. Now there were only seven seconds remaining, and the Colts were on the Giants' 7 with not enough time for another pass. Steve Myhra came in to try a field goal. The Giant defense braced to block the kick, but the ball sailed through the uprights at the final gun. After sixty brutal minutes, they had played to a 17–17 tie.

But there are no ties when the world championship is at stake. Never before had there been a sudden-death overtime in an NFL championship game, but there would be one now under the lights at Yankee Stadium. Sudden death. The first team to score in any manner would be crowned world champions of 1958.

The Giants received the kickoff, and now it was the Colts' turn to get stubborn and proud on defense. They held the Giants, forcing them to kick, and the Colts put the ball in play on their own 20-yard line. The Colts had the ball for thirteen plays . . . thirteen plays that will live in infamy in the history of the New York Giants . . . thirteen plays that will be remembered and replayed for as long as there is football in Baltimore.

It started simply enough. L. G. Dupre scoots right end for ten yards and a first down, then an incomplete pass, then Dupre up the middle for three. A safety valve pass to fullback Alan Ameche gives the Colts a first down on their 40, and Dupre goes around right end for seven.

Unitas then tries to pass and is hit for a twelve-yard loss. But on the next play, scrambling to avoid tacklers, he hits Berry for a first down on the Giants' 42. Now the Colts are moving and the fans are hushed, sensing what is happening. Unitas is moving in for the kill like a fearless matador. He checks off at the line of scrimmage and sends Ameche up the vacated middle for a first down to the Giants' 23, but Dupre is then stopped for no gain. Unitas goes to the air, hitting Berry on a slant to the Giants' 8.

He is within field goal range, and three points will win it just the same as six. But Unitas sends Ameche up the middle for a gain of one. It is second and goal to go on the seven and here, on the twelfth play, Unitas turns gambler. He could keep the ball on the ground, protecting it for the certain field goal. Instead, he throws to Jim Mutscheller on the right flat, who makes the catch and is dropped on the one.

Third down and goal to go from the one. Unitas calls his thirteenth play, a blast inside right tackle by Ameche. Touchdown! The Baltimore Colts are world champions! The quarterback who cost 80¢ has marched them to a victory worth $4,700 per man, an incredible 5,875 to 1 shot.

But that was not to be the end of it. Not yet. Reporters swarmed into the Colts' dressing room, surrounding Unitas.

They all wanted to know the same thing: why did he risk passing to Mutscheller on the twelfth play of the drive when all he needed to win was a field goal? Wasn't he afraid of some Giant intercepting the ball and dashing all the way down the sideline for a touchdown?

Unitas knew that question would come. He had expected it. And he knew how he would answer because there was only one answer. He paused to think because he wanted to say it just right. "When you know what you're doing," he said, "they're not intercepted."

He knew, too, that people would not understand the answer. It sounded cocky, conceited. But it wasn't, really, although it was egotistical, because Johnny Unitas possesses the egotism of greatness.

But how could he explain it to them so they would understand the egotism of the remark? How could he tell them of all the hard knocks, which did not make him soft, but made him tough? How could he tell them of his father dying when Johnny was five and of working on the coal truck as a kid? Of being rejected at Notre Dame and being unwanted by the Pittsburgh Steelers?

How could he tell them of working on a piledriver and playing football for $6 a game on a bed of rocks? How could he tell them of the hard work and the struggle and the sweat and the pain he suffered to perfect his skills for this season, this game, this play?

And how could he make them see that it had all come out of him on that one pass to Jim Mutscheller—the desire, the determination, the confidence, the perseverance, the guts, the courage. All the things that go to make up this man called Johnny Unitas.

ELGIN BAYLOR

"The time is now. You have to find out once and for all."

It was heartbreaking to watch him. It was like looking at a faded and tattered old snapshot of a loved one taken in the dim and distant past. There was no mistaking the identity. The smooth, effortless grace, the powerful shoulders and arms, the thick neck, the massive thighs, the familiar nervous twitch. This was Elgin Baylor of the Los Angeles

Lakers, considered by many to be the greatest all-around performer ever to play the game of basketball.

But this was not that Elgin Baylor. Gone was the explosive speed that left opponents trailing in futile pursuit. Gone were the incredible moves, the pivoting, starting, stopping, twisting, dashing, leaping, stretching, bounding that made him so magnificent to watch and so impossible to defend.

"Take a vacation, bum. Do us all a favor," had come the cruel suggestion from a courtside loudmouth, some unthinking, unfeeling ingrate of such short memory.

It was November 1963 and Elgin Baylor had scored eight points in a game against the St. Louis Hawks. Elgin Baylor scoring eight points in a game? It was impossible. It was more unbelievable than Wilt Chamberlain scoring a hundred. Elgin Baylor had not scored a mere eight points in a game since he was a kid playing in schoolyards in Washington, D.C. There was no way Elgin Baylor could score only eight points in a game . . . but there was a way . . . only one way.

He was playing on crippled legs. He looked suddenly old and weary. Watching him was like seeing a person running in a dream, taking long, graceful strides but going nowhere. It was like watching a once-great tenor gone bad, mouthing the same words but without the tone.

The pain in Baylor's legs was unbearable, but it was not just the pain that had turned him into a faded memory of the great ballplayer he once was. If he could do the things he had done before he would do them, even with the pain. But movement itself was restricted. He had been to the Mayo Clinic in Rochester, Minnesota, before the season. They did everything to try to find the cause of his pain. They dug needles into his aching knees and took series after series of X rays and tests, but in the end they could not agree on their diagnoses and he was sent home. It was either calcium deposits above the knee or a bone growth, but they agreed on one thing—it was serious. It was a condition that probably would never get any better. It might not get worse, but certainly no better.

Now frustration and humiliation were heaped on top of the pain as he struggled to regain something close to the skills he once possessed. After the pitiful showing against St. Louis, he was held to a paltry thirteen points against the Celtics. Playing the Baltimore Bullets he took 21 shots and made 3, scoring only 10 points in the game.

"I'm just sick about it," said his friend and teammate, Jerry West. "This is a hard thing to watch. Elg is one of the finest men in the world and the best player I ever saw. To see him crippled and scoring less points than some of the subs on the other team just makes you want to cry."

Rumors flew all around the National Basketball Association that Elgin Baylor, playing on gimpy legs, had come to the end of his fabulous career. One reporter was even so bold as to ask Baylor if he felt the end might be at hand for him. In an uncharacteristic display of temper, Baylor took out his frustration and his pain on that reporter. "I have no time to talk to gravediggers," he roared.

Yet even Baylor had begun to hear the rumors and even he had to wonder how much longer he could go on enduring the pain in his knees and the embarrassment of scoring ten points a game, barely one-third of his normal output. His wife, Ruby, begged him to come home and rest, to miss a few games and try to build up the strength in his legs.

"I can't, Ruby," Elgin replied. "We're only a game ahead of St. Louis. If we can pull out in front, I'll think about resting. I've got to play for these people for all they've done for me. I'd play with a hand cut off if it will help them."

Often he had played when he should have rested, motivated by a loyalty that is quite uncommon among professional athletes. In 1960 Baylor leaped for a rebound and caught the third finger of his right hand on the netting, almost severing the finger. Doctors urged him to sit out a few games, fearful that further injury would permanently damage the hand, but Baylor refused to rest. He knew he was needed on the floor and at the box office, so he had the finger fitted with a protective steel plate. He played with the bad finger for four weeks, averaging better than thirty points a game in that time.

Basketball and the Lakers did a lot for Elgin, but no more than he did for them. He saved the franchise, and the Lakers appreciated it and took care of him, but he worked hard and earned everything he got. It never came easy for Baylor. He had to struggle to get where he did.

It is said that when his fifth child came into the world, John Baylor of Washington, D.C., took out his gold pocket watch, the one with the long gold chain, to check the time of this wonderful event. It was an Elgin watch and it was John Baylor's most prized possession. He decided to name this prized child after the watch.

Young Elgin grew big and strong. At Phelps Vocational High School in Washington, he played basketball
and was named to the all-city team his first two years. But
Elgin was not happy. He was a shy boy and he retreated
from the sudden attention being showered upon him because of his basketball ability. He was something of a
celebrity in his neighborhood, but it was a fame he did not
seek and did not want. There was only one way to escape
from the spotlight—he quit school and went to work as a
checker in a furniture store.

After a year, his mother convinced Elgin to return to
school. He entered Springarn High, an academic, Negro
high school. He was more mature, better able to cope with
the attention he received when he set a District of Columbia
schoolboy scoring record by pouring in 68 points in one
game. He was the first Negro ever named to the all-metro-
politan team in basketball, and he raised the eyebrows of
college coaches all over the East.

But Elgin's two years in a vocational school and his
total aversion to studies forced most colleges to discount
him as a prospect. He followed a high school chum to the
College of Idaho, a tiny school of 450 students in Cardwell,
Idaho. He went as a football player, but his basketball
ability was so evident that Sam Vokes, who coached both
football and basketball, decided Elgin should not waste his
talents and risk injury on the football field. It was not long
before Baylor was getting the same kind of attention and
recognition at the College of Idaho that had disturbed him
so much at Phelps Vocational.

After he had spent a year at college, the administra-
tion decided to deemphasize its athletic program and fired

coach Vokes, who planned to take Elgin with him when he landed another job. Meanwhile, Elgin had been contacted by a wealthy automobile salesman from Seattle, who wondered if Baylor might consider transferring to the University of Seattle. When Elgin expressed interest, the automobile salesman sent his private plane to pick up Elgin and take him to the Seattle campus. Baylor fell in love with the beauty of the Northwest, and the following fall he enrolled at Seattle University.

He had to sit out a year, but during the next two seasons he propelled Seattle into collegiate basketball prominence, almost single-handedly putting the Chieftains into contention for the national championship. In his first year at Seattle he finished third in the country in scoring with a 29.7 average, and he was the nation's leading rebounder as Seattle finished with a 22–3 record.

The following year the Chieftains went all the way to the NCAA finals, losing to Kentucky. With 32.5 points per game for the season, Baylor finished second in scoring to Oscar Robertson and third in rebounding.

Baylor still had a year of varsity eligibility remaining, but he also became eligible for the professional draft. When he was selected on the first round by the Minneapolis Lakers and offered a $20,000 contract to sign, Elgin decided to take the money and turn pro.

Ever since George Mikan had retired, the once-powerful Lakers had been experiencing difficult times. Attendance was quickly spiralling downward when Baylor joined the team in the fall of 1958. In his first game he scored the Lakers' first 6 points and went on to hit 25 for the game.

It might have been an omen, for Elgin averaged 24.9 points per game in his rookie season, fourth highest in the league behind veterans Bob Pettit of St. Louis, Jack Twyman of Cincinnati and Paul Arizin of Philadelphia. Baylor also had the season's game high of 55 points, which he scored against the Cincinnati Royals. More remarkable, however, were his 1,050 rebounds considering that, at 6'5", Elgin was practically a pygmy among the huge sequoias that inhabit the National Basketball Association. Baylor helped the Lakers advance to the finals of the league playoffs. The following year he averaged 29.6 points a game, finishing third in the league behind Wilt Chamberlain and Twyman.

The Lakers had been on the verge of bankruptcy before Baylor arrived, but he revived interest in the team, enabling it to hang on until they moved to Los Angeles and a brand new sports arena in 1960.

Baylor was a smash hit on the West Coast, averaging 34.8, 38.2 and 34.0 in his first three years there. Angelenos, who had never seen professional basketball, were seeing it at its very best with Elgin Baylor and Jerry West playing for the home side. Baylor was to basketball in Los Angeles what Sandy Koufax was to baseball, and owner Bob Short could point his finger at Elgin as the man who not only saved his franchise in Minneapolis, but helped it flourish in Los Angeles.

Elgin became one of the game's great superstars. He was magnificent to watch, his powerful, graceful body soaring into the air to float a soft jump shot into the nets. And he was immediately recognizable by his famous twitch, which made it appear he was trying to bury his head into his shoulder. Curiously, the twitch disappeared when he was not on the court. It was, obviously, a manifestation of the fierce competive fires that burned within him.

In his first five years as a professional, Baylor averaged better than 32 points a game; set a record for most points in a playoff game by scoring 61 against the Boston Celtics in 1962; broke the single game, regular season scoring record with 64 points against Boston in 1959, and raised that record to 71 a year later against the New York Knickerbockers.

"Inch for inch," raved Los Angeles coach Fred Schaus, "he is the greatest player in the game. If there is money on the table, I'd take Elg over anybody."

Baylor's superstar performances on the court made their impression at the gate. The Lakers became the first team in NBA history to gross over $1 million in a single season. The club made a survey in which it established that Elgin's presence in the lineup guaranteed about 2,000 more fans per game. That meant his value to the team was $6,000 per game and $200,000 per season; in his first three seasons Baylor had personally put close to three-quarters of a million dollars into the Lakers' treasury.

Owner Short showed his gratitude to Elgin after the 1961 season by signing him to a five-year contract that would bring him $250,000 whether he played or not. But, as he limped through the 1963–64 season, it appeared Elgin would be unable to fulfill the contract as an active player.

After the 1964 season, Baylor put himself completely in the hands of the famed Los Angeles orthopedic surgeon,

Dr. Robert Kerlan. It was Dr. Kerlan who had cured the
mysterious circulatory ailment in Sandy Koufax's left
hand; it was Dr. Kerlan who had treated Koufax so that
he might pitch with arthritis in his left elbow; it was Dr.
Kerlan who had repaired Maury Wills' damaged knee, and
it was Dr. Kerlan who examined Baylor and said: "His
problem isn't in his knees at all. Some deposits, possibly
of the calcium type, have built in the quadriceps group,
which is a linkage of tendon and muscle above the knee."
Surgery, said Dr. Kerlan, would not be necessary. Instead,
he prescribed treatment with a vasculator machine, hoping
to work out the condition with massage.

Every day during the summer of 1964, Baylor met
with Dr. Kerlan for his massage, and when the summer was
over, Dr. Kerlan sent Elgin out to play. Determination and
hard work paid off. Baylor played through the entire 1964–
1965 season and, although it was not an altogether painless
season, his knees were vastly improved. He missed only six
games and boosted his scoring average to 27.1, fourth best
in the league. He had showed them that he was not through
yet.

Los Angeles won the Western Division Championship
and met the Baltimore Bullets in the first round of the league
play-offs. The first game was just five minutes old when Baylor went up for one of his patented jump shots and came
down with a shock. He felt a pull in his left knee, and the
pain was so severe that he had to be taken out of the game.

Dr. Kerlan operated the very next day. The patella, the
bone which holds the kneecap in place, had been torn
free of the kneecap and had to be sewn back in place.

It was a rare injury and a delicate operation, and there could be no guarantee that Elgin would ever have normal use of his knee again, let alone play basketball on it.

The summer of 1965 was like a long, unending nightmare for Baylor. He went to see Dr. Kerlan religiously for therapy, but there was little improvement in his knee. He could barely walk, and the pain practically made him cry out in anguish. He had just about given up hope of ever playing again when suddenly, miraculously, the pain vanished, the knee improved and felt strong again. To everyone's surprse, Baylor was in the starting lineup when the season opened in October 1965.

But caution and fear gripped Baylor. He played carefully, never going all out. He had never had a broken bone before. He had cuts and bruises and calcium deposits and excruciating pain, but never a broken bone. He didn't know what to expect or how to protect it, so he tried to keep the pressure off his left knee. In so doing, he put added pressure on the right knee. He punished it so severely that it could not withstand the stress. The calcium flared up again, bringing terrible pain once more. "My legs hurt so," Baylor complained, "that when I woke up in the morning I could tell if it was raining or not just by the way they felt."

Late in November Baylor could take the pain no longer. He went to Dr. Kerlan, who put the right leg in a cast for a month. When the cast was removed and Baylor returned to the lineup, he was of little help to the team. He was terribly out of shape, still in pain, and more fearful and cautious than ever of reinjuring either of his legs. There was a month left in the season. Baylor was averaging twelve

Elgin's bad knees often forced him to warm the bench in frustration.

points a game and doing the Lakers very little good. Dr. Kerlan summoned him to his office.

"Look, Elgin," Dr. Kerlan said, "the time is now. You have to find out for once and for all. You either have to go out there and test it by playing all out or forget about playing basketball and come here and rest with me. Which will it be?"

Elgin decided to test it. He decided to forget all about the pain and the fear of further injury and go all out. There were less than twenty games left. For those few remaining games, Baylor played daringly, fearlessly. He averaged 25 points and 14 rebounds a game as the Lakers again won the Western Division title.

Baylor's season average of 16.6 was not to be considered a measure of his ability, nor was it indicative of the kind of ball he was playing as the Lakers met the St. Louis Hawks in the semifinal round of the play-offs.

It was a new season for Elgin Baylor and it started on April 1, 1966, in Los Angeles. In the first playoff game, he scored 22 points and grabbed 15 rebounds as the Lakers defeated the Hawks 129–106. The Lakers won the second game, too, and once again it was Baylor who led the way with 14 rebounds, 9 assists and 42 points. After six games the two teams were even at three games apiece. In the seventh game, the one the Lakers had to win to stay alive, Baylor scored 33 points to lead his team to a 130–121 victory. The Lakers went into the finals against the heavily favored defending world champions, the Boston Celtics.

On the surface it was the Los Angeles Lakers against the Boston Celtics, but in reality it was a clash of two men with enormous pride. It was Red Auerbach, hoping to bow out as Celtic coach as a winner with his eighth consecutive world championship; proud of his record, proud of his team and proud of the Celtic defense. But he still remembered the 61 points scored by Elgin Baylor in 1962—

which remained in the books as a play-off record for a single game—and he was fearful of the same thing happening again.

Pitted against Auerbach was Elgin Baylor, trying to prove to the world that he was not finished; hungry to play on a world championship team for the first time in his career, and fully realizing that this might be his last opportunity to do so. It seemed Baylor had taken this play-off as his own personal challenge. He scored 36 points and grabbed 20 rebounds, giving the Lakers the impetus to defeat the Celtics in overtime in the first game, 133–129.

But the irrepressible Celtics do not quit that easily. They came fighting back to take the next three games, and it seemed they would put a sudden and decisive end to the 1966 season.

Faced with elimination, it was the Lakers' turn to come storming back. It was their crippled superstar, Elgin Baylor, who led them. He pumped in 41 points and picked off 16 rebounds in the fifth game, and he scored 25 points and grabbed 14 rebounds in the sixth game. The series was even, three games apiece. It all came down to the final game in Boston on April 28. One game to decide if it were going to be a magnificent farewell for Red Auerbach or a glorious comeback for Elgin Baylor.

It was a few minutes after seven at night and the Lakers were dressing for their date with destiny. They could hear the crowd outside, impatient, apprehensive, beginning to grow excited with anticipation for what lay ahead.

Inside, in a tiny, crammed dressing room, the Lakers were impatient and apprehensive too; they also were

beginning to grow excited with anticipation. What lay ahead
was a great opportunity . . . to beat the Boston Celtics, the
best in the business, in their own arena, before their home
fans and to become champions of all the basketball world.

They spoke very little, because to speak might betray
the tension that was in each of them. Not even coach Schaus
had very much to say at the pre-game meeting. What was
there to say? They were all professionals, they had been
through this before, they had played against these Celtics
many times. They knew what to do; they just had to do it.

In the quiet of the dressing room, Elgin Baylor was left
with his thoughts. All the triumph and pain, all the successes
and failures, all the glory and anguish of the last decade
streaked through his mind. Just six months before everybody
said it was over for him. They taunted and jeered and wrote
him off in the newspapers. And Elgin Baylor believed what
they wrote. He believed it not because they wrote it, but
because of the pain that raged in his legs, and because of the
frustration of not being able to do the things he had done so
mechanically before. But he had come back, he had showed
them, and now, sitting in that quiet, crowded dressing room,
feeling the tension well up within him, Elgin Baylor hoped
for the energy to do it just one more time.

He went out to meet the Boston Celtics in the seventh
game of the NBA championship play-off. He gave it every
ounce of strength and courage he possessed. But it was not
enough.

The seventh game was all defense, and when it was
defense it was always the Boston Celtics. They opened a
huge lead in the fourth period and they held on as the

Lakers tried desperately to fight back. But, in the end, the Lakers fell two points short. The Boston Celtics were world champions once again.

Elgin Baylor had lost the battle, the battle to embellish his comeback by playing on his first world championship team. But he had won an even bigger battle. He had won the battle over pain and fear.

GIANTS 7 23 24 30 6 12 14 15 44
LF RF CF 1B C 3B 2B SS
BALL
ODGERS 3 19 6 12 29 25 8 44 32
CF 3B 1B LF 2B RF C SS P
STRIKE
1 2 3 4 5 6 7 8 9 10 R H E
OUT 2
GIANTS 0 0 0 0 0 0 0 0 0 0 0
ODGERS 0 1 0 0 0 3 0 4 8 12 0
20 3 2 12
UMPIRES

SANDY KOUFAX

"Yeah, some sore elbow. It's sore except between the first and ninth innings."

The huge room overflowed with reporters. There were more than one hundred of them, representing all media of the press. They knew exactly why they had been summoned to this hastily called press conference. They knew, and yet, somehow, they still could not believe it was happening.

The clock on the wall said 1:08 when he entered the
room. He was strikingly handsome, meticulously dressed
and he walked with an athlete's grace and confidence. His
black, wavy hair, streaked with gray and slightly receding,
was combed neatly in place. He wore a royal-blue sports
coat, black slacks, black slip-on shoes and a black tie in a
windsor knot that fit neatly in the inverted V of his white,
button-down collar. He was the picture of affluence, the
image of health and youthful vigor. As he sat at the table,
upon which fifteen microphones had been heaped, he had
the look of a movie star about to discuss his latest picture
or a young executive about to reveal the terms of a new
business deal.

When he spoke his voice was deep, resonant, clear and
unemotional. He said, simply: "I have just a short statement
to make. A few minutes ago I sent Buzzie Bavasi a letter
asking him to put me on the voluntary retired list."

That was all. Just like that it was over. They all had
known what was coming, yet for a brief instant the room
was quiet. Then it came alive, with flashbulbs popping and
reporters buzzing excitedly and shouting questions at the
young man and scurrying to telephones to call newspaper
offices with the story. It was all over. The end of the line. He
had been the greatest and now it was over and it was hard to
believe. Still young and at the peak of his success, Sandy
Koufax had retired from baseball.

The room was plush, expensively furnished and crammed with reporters who were there to record this event. This
is what Sandy Koufax had become in just a few years.
These were the surroundings and this was the attention he

had come to deserve. It ended in elegance. This was not at all the way it had started.

It began on a dusty sandlot in the Coney Island section of Brooklyn. It started with a team called the Parkviews and an injured pitcher whose name would have little meaning today even if it could be remembered. It started with the manager of the Parkviews talking to his first baseman, a tall, dark-haired kid. "You pitch today, Sandy. You've got the strongest arm on the team."

So Sandy Koufax pitched, and it was not exactly like finding a pearl in a plate of oysters, but it was good enough for Sandy to pitch again . . . and again . . . and again . . . and to be pitching on a day when a Brooklyn sportswriter named Jimmy Murphy happened to be sitting in the stands. Murphy had been a semi-pro pitcher in his younger days, and he noticed in Koufax' throwing a kind of unharnessed fury. He reported his discovery to the Brooklyn Dodgers, and the Dodgers said they would check out the big left-handed pitcher from the Parkviews.

Sandy went on to the University of Cincinnati that fall. Not much was heard about him until December 1954, when the Dodgers issued a short publicity release. It stated that they had signed a left-handed pitcher from Brooklyn to a bonus contract. It said the boy's name was Sandy Koufax. A lot of people wondered if this was somebody's idea of a joke.

Koufax had gained some measure of prominence as an athlete at Brooklyn's Lafayette High School, but it was as a basketball player. Somebody remembered he had once worked out against the New York Knickerbockers and jumped center against Harry Gallatin. Gallatin had said: "This kid's good. He'll be in our league someday." Somebody remembered, too, that he had played on the Lafayette baseball team as a first baseman. Sandy Koufax a pitcher? Even his best friends didn't know.

According to the quaint rule of servitude then in effect, any player signed for a bonus in excess of $4,000 had to spend at least two seasons in the major leagues before being farmed out. Baseball lost more great prospects that way; Sandy Koufax almost was one of them. He had received a bonus of $14,000, and so he went to spring training as a Brooklyn Dodger in 1955, with the sum total of less than 25 games' experience as a pitcher. It was not the happiest of springs for Sandy. While the Dodgers were getting ready for another National League dogfight, Sandy was trying to learn how to properly stand on the pitcher's mound and was hoping to become acquainted with home plate. "Hitting· against him that spring," one Dodger veteran said, "was like playing Russian roulette with five bullets."

Koufax, they said, could throw his blazing fastball through a brick wall—if he could hit the brick wall. The Dodgers spent hours working with him, but there was little improvement. Even warming up he threw the ball everywhere except in the catcher's glove.

Frustration turned to humiliation; improvement came agonizingly slowly, and Sandy's rookie season was one of long, idle torture. The Dodgers were fighting for the National League pennant. Koufax felt more like a spectator than a participant as he watched Jackie Robinson, Pee Wee Reese, Duke Snider, Gil Hodges, Don Newcombe, Carl

Erskine and the other great Dodger stars sweep through the league spreading destruction and fear. Koufax wore the same uniform as they did, but he did not feel like one of them.

It was not until the Dodgers' 66th game of the season that Sandy got his name in a major league box score for the first time. It was a debut the world will little note nor long remember.

The Dodgers were leading the league by fourteen games when Koufax walked in from the bullpen the night of June 24, 1955, in Milwaukee. The Braves were leading 7–1. Koufax pitched two innings and, although the first three men he faced got on base, he survived without allowing a run. Nobody compared him to Walter Johnson.

The Dodgers easily won the pennant and the World Series in 1955, beating the hated New York Yankees in seven games. In the clubhouse following the seventh game, while the others rejoiced in victory—swilling champagne, pouring it over each other, tearing at one another's clothes, shouting, cheering and pounding one another joyously—young Koufax remained off to the side, in the corner of the room, feeling he had not earned the right to be a part of the madly wild celebration. His entire contribution for the season had been 12 games, 42 innings, 2 victories, 2 defeats, 30 strikeouts and 28 walks.

The following year was hardly better. He appeared in 16 games, pitched 59 innings, won 2, lost 4, struck out 30 and walked 29. Again the Dodgers won the National League pennant, and again Koufax felt like an intruder, a gate-crasher at a private party.

As old Dodger heroes vanished and opportunity increased, Koufax got more chances to pitch. He became a part of the team. At last he belonged, but there was little satisfaction because he belonged to failure as the Dodgers' grasp slipped and they lost the hold they once had on the National League. Frustration and humiliation were slowly changing to discouragment, as Koufax despaired of ever being able to put all his talents together. There were tantalizing moments, moments when it appeared he had found the answer. There was the time in 1955, his rookie year, when he was given a start and he shut out the Cincinnati Reds, striking out 14; there was the night of August 31, 1959, when he set a National League record and tied Bob Feller's major league record by striking out 18 men in a game against the Giants; there was the 1–0 defeat in the 1959 World Series against the Chicago White Sox, the winning run scoring on a double play. But each time it was only a false promise of greatness and it never really happened for him. After six years in the big leagues, he had won only 36 games and lost 40. He had struck out 683 batters, but he had walked 405, and not even the change of scenery when the Dodgers moved across the country from Brooklyn to Los Angeles had helped.

Koufax was depressed. The thought of quitting passed quickly through his mind . . . and just as quickly it passed out. Baseball was the only thing he knew. What else could he do? He asked Dodger general manager Buzzie Bavasi to trade him, figuring a change would help, but Bavasi refused. Koufax was just 25 years old and the Dodgers hoped that someday, somewhere, somehow it would all come to him.

It happened suddenly, unexpectedly, one day in the spring of 1961. The Dodgers had sent Koufax to pitch in a "B" squad game and, on the bus going to the game, Sandy was sitting next to his friend, catcher Norm Sherry.

"This game doesn't mean too much, Sandy," Sherry said. "I'd like you to try something."

"What would you like me to try?" Sandy asked.

"I've always thought your trouble was that you try to throw the ball too hard and that's why you can't get the ball over the plate. Just for today, try not to throw so hard. You've got good enough stuff to get hitters out without trying to overpower them. If you let up a little you're sure to have better control."

"Okay, I'll try it," Sandy agreed.

The result was amazing. Norm Sherry was right. Sandy was throwing easily, not trying to overpower the hitters, and he was still throwing the ball by them. What's more, by letting up just a little, he found he was able to get the ball over the plate. He tingled with excitement as he breezed through the hitters. He was convinced that at long last he had found the answer.

He maintained the pattern suggested by Sherry all through the 1961 season and the results were incredible. He won eighteen games and lost thirteen. He set a National League record by striking out 269 batters and, best of all, he walked only 96 in 256 innings. He was suddenly a star. Around the league they began to talk in awesome tones about the young Dodger left-hander who had finally found himself. They raved about his blazing fast ball and crackling curve, and they expressed astonishment at his new-found control. Veteran baseball men nodded knowingly when the name Sandy Koufax was mentioned. "Always knew he'd make it some day," they said, sagely. "He always had great stuff. All he had to do was learn control."

All he had to do was learn control! There were hundreds of pitchers through the years who "always had great stuff" and "all they had to do was learn control." But they never learned it. It is not something you buy at the local supermarket. You do not wake up one morning and suddenly have control. You get it by practice. You get it by pitching and experimenting and eliminating problems. You get it by perseverance and long hours of hard, frustrating work. It took seven years for Sandy Koufax to learn control; seven years for him to become an overnight sensation.

His problems all behind him, Koufax looked ahead to the 1962 season with hope and confidence, emotions he had never before experienced. He was not disappointed, nor was he disappointing.

On April 24 against the Chicago Cubs he became the first pitcher in baseball history to strike out eighteen batters in each of two games. Two months later he pitched his first no-hit, no-run game. It was against the New York Mets, and was one of the most overpowering pitching performances ever witnessed. "Either he throws the fastest ball I've ever seen," said an amazed Richie Ashburn, "or I'm going blind."

By the all-star break the name Sandy Koufax was synonymous with pitching excellence. He had won fourteen games and was on his way to a record for strikeouts when, suddenly, disaster struck. His career was in jeopardy. It happened totally without warning. At first there was a numbness in the tip of his left index finger. Then the finger began to blister. Then it peeled and became red and raw. Sandy refused to become alarmed. Stubbornly, he concealed the injury until it began to affect his pitching, until he could no longer grip the ball properly. By then it was almost too late.

At first the doctors thought Sandy might lose the finger. He was suffering from a rare circulatory ailment known as Raynaud's Phenomenon. Something had blocked off the circulation of blood flowing to his left hand. Sandy thought it might have developed when he was struck on the pitching hand while batting earlier in the year. Doctors, however, attributed it to the unusually overdeveloped muscles in his left shoulder. When he drew his arm back to pitch, they reasoned, the thickly bunched muscles temporarily blocked off the flow of blood to his hand.

Sandy remembered a time, back in 1959, when he suffered shoulder pains and missed a month of the season. At the time, it was decided the only way to work out the soreness was to pitch despite the pain. It was painful for him to throw and it was painful for others to watch.

"How do you feel?" a teammate asked after Koufax had pitched a half hour of batting practice.

"Good," he replied.

"But you were grimacing every time you threw."

"That's nothing," Sandy said. "I usually cry."

The shoulder injury in 1959 hardly caused much of a ripple in the baseball ocean. But now Koufax was on the verge of becoming the best pitcher in the game, and his finger was the center of nationwide attention. He was put through a series of examinations and X rays. The finger was treated with shots, drugs, ointments and simple massage. But Sandy was finished with pitching for the year at least. He sat on the sidelines, his future in doubt, watching his teammates lose the 1962 pennant to the San Francisco Giants in a play-off and unable to lift a finger to help.

Doctors saved his finger and restored the flow of blood, but there would be no way of knowing if recovery was complete until he pitched in 1963. It was not long before he had erased the doubts and eased the troubled minds of his bosses and Dodger teammates.

On the second day of the season he beat the Cubs, 2–1, with a five-hitter. Two starts later he beat the Cubs again, this time shutting them out and striking out fourteen. Two starts later he pitched his second no-hitter, this time against the Giants, a much more formidable opponent that the victims of his first no-hitter.

No pitcher in the last thirty years had a year like Sandy Koufax had in 1963. He won 25 games and lost only 5. He broke his own strikeout record by fanning 306 batters, and he walked only 58 in 311 innings. He led the National League with an earned run average of 1.88. He won both the Most Valuable Player award and the Cy Young Award. But his greatest hour was yet to come.

It was October 2, the opening game of the 1963 World Series in New York's Yankee Stadium. In the bottom of the first inning, Koufax started by striking out Tony Kubek. Then he struck out Bobby Richardson and Tom Tresh. In the second inning he struck out Mickey Mantle and Roger Maris. He had struck out the first five Yankees he faced and, for the remainder of the game, he would have most of the 69,000 fans on their feet, screaming, stamping and cheering the New York boy pitching for the visitors from Los Angeles.

In the eighth inning he struck out Bobby Richardson again. It was his fourteenth strikeout, tying the World Series record held by former Dodger Carl Erskine and set in the same ballpark just ten years before. Sandy still had a full inning, three more chances to break the record, but he failed to get a strikeout in his first two outs. Then he faced pinch hitter Harry Bright. With the count two and two he threw his devastating curve ball. Bright took it for strike three . . . and the record.

The Dodgers won that first game, 5–2. They also won the second and third games, and, in the fourth game, Koufax pitched again. He struck out eight and allowed six hits as the Dodgers won, 2–1. They had swept the World Series in four games.

No ballplayer ever captured the imagination of the public as the handsome, dark-haired, Brooklyn-born bachelor did that year. After the World Series he was in constant demand for endorsements and appearances and, although he tried to maintain a closely guarded privacy, stories and pictures of him accepting some award appeared in the newspapers practically every day during the winter. He was America's newest idol. Everyone had flipped for him. Sandy was a model and a modest hero. He was kind, decent, pleasant, humble, patient and cooperative in the face of constant demands on his time. He wore his success well, but then he had had a long time to prepare for it.

No player so dominated the game as Koufax did during the few years he was at his peak. His very presence on the mound turned the Dodgers from mediocrity to excel-

lence; from a string quartet to a concert; from a plain Jane
to a ravishing beauty queen. All over the National League
they came in droves to see him pitch. Whenever he pitched,
10,000 more people came to the game, bought tickets,
parked their cars, drank beer and soda pop, ate hot dogs and
peanuts, bought pennants and souvenirs and, having enjoyed
themselves, decided to come back again. He was a left-
handed money-making machine.

When he pitched the Dodgers almost never lost. When
he pitched for an entire season, the Dodgers won the pennant. When he did not, they did not, which became painfully evident in 1964.

The year started out like most others. There was a
shoulder injury early in the season and a cold wave of fear
running through the Dodgers as Koufax struggled to regain
his form. Then it was June 4 in Philadelphia. He had won
five games and lost four when he went out to pitch against
the Phillies with rumors swirling all around him that he had
never fully recovered from the shoulder injury. He ended
the rumors that night. He ended them in typical Koufax
fashion—dramatically and spectacularly. He pitched his
third no-hitter, and through all the years of baseball, in all
the pages of the record books, only four other pitchers had
ever pitched three no-hitters.

It was all right after that. He was the Sandy Koufax of
old; the great Sandy Koufax; the dominant, crowd-pulling,
certain-victory Sandy Koufax.

Then, on August 8 in Milwaukee, he slid into second
base and landed hard on his left elbow. He felt the shock
clear down to his spiked shoes. He finished the game

and beat the Braves, 2–1, but when he awoke the next morning he had a companion. It was a lump on his elbow the size of a grapefruit, almost as if it were an extension of his arm.

He told no one about the lump, waiting to see what would happen. A lifetime of bumps and bruises, aches and pains had taught him it was useless to run to a doctor with each little pain. He went about his normal routine, normal only for a major league pitcher. Curiously, he found that the swelling and pain disappeared when he pitched, only to return after he had pitched. The solution was quite obvious. He continued to pitch, almost in self defense. And from the way he threw, his problems were minor compared to those of the hitters who faced him. He won his nineteenth game of the season—his fifteenth in his last sixteen decisions—and the next morning he awoke to find his arm filled with fluid and swollen twice its normal size. This time he went immediately to Dr. Robert Kerlan, the orthopedic surgeon who is one of the Dodgers' team physicians.

X rays were taken. It was discovered that Sandy had developed traumatic arthritis in his left elbow. This condition had been coming on for years and had been hastened by the shock in Milwaukee. It was easy enough to reduce the swelling, to ease the pain and arrest the arthritis. The fluid was drawn out with a needle, the inflammation was treated with injections of cortisone and pills, but Dr. Kerlan decided it was best for Sandy to forget about pitching for the remainder of the year. He did. Predictably, the Dodgers finished down the ladder in the National League standings.

There was nothing further that could be done during the winter of 1964. The off-season was a time of hoping and waiting to try the arm again in the spring of 1965. There was no doubt about the diagnosis—Sandy Koufax had arthritis and it could not be cured, but it could be controlled. There was a chance, with the proper precautions and treatment, that Sandy would be able to pitch in 1965. But the continued strain on his arm would only worsen the condition.

Eagerly, Koufax tested the arm as soon as he could that spring. He found, to his surprise, that he was pitching without pain. More surprising and more encouraging was the absence of any swelling after he had pitched. But the joy was short-lived. Three weeks before the opening of the season, Sandy pitched and the arm swelled. He was back where he started—in Dr. Kerlan's office. More treatment led to the conclusion that the swelling could be reduced with a dose of cortisone shot directly into the elbow.

Koufax was back two days before opening day, pitching three innings against the Washington Senators in an exhibition game. He was convinced that shots and medication could help him limp through the season. His first start came in the fourth game of that 1965 season. Although struggling because of lack of work, he won 6–2 against the Phillies, and all of Los Angeles breathed a sigh of relief.

It was a year to remember. On August 10 Sandy won his twentieth game against only four defeats and the world laughed at the thought of this magnificent pitcher being an arthritic.

"Yeah, some sore elbow," scoffed Cincinnati manager Dick Sisler. "It's sore except between the first and ninth innings."

They laughed, but they saw only the results, only the wins or losses in the box scores. They didn't know that he had abandoned the slider, often could not throw the curve ball because of the pain, and had to get by with just fast balls and change-ups. They didn't know of the swelling and

An exhausted Koufax goes through the post-game ritual of soaking his arm in ice.

United Press International Photo

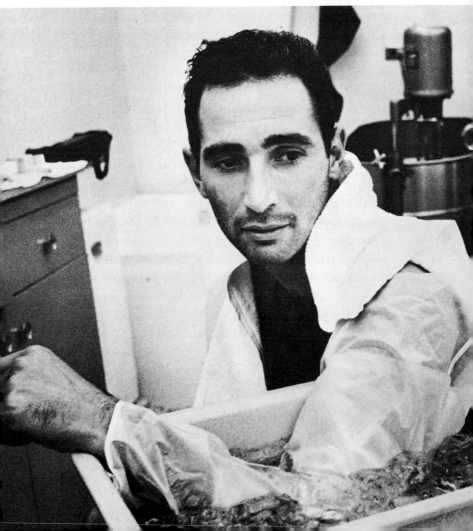

the pain, and they didn't see the ritual of cortisone shot, oral medication, heat and ice bath which Koufax followed religiously before and after every game. Still, by some miracle, he was defying medical science. As long as he was willing to let them use his arm for a pincushion and to subsist on a diet of pills, the arm would respond long enough for him to pitch for three hours every fourth day.

And then, on September 9, 1965, he gave the world good cause to laugh at his troubles. On that night he made a mockery of medical science. He put the crowning touch on his magnificent career.

Sandy had lost three straight games as he took the mound at Dodger Stadium that night. The Dodgers were involved in another of their typical, torrid pennant fights, just one-half game behind the Giants. As the days dwindled down to the end of the season, each victory was precious, each defeat painful.

For four innings Koufax and the Cubs' lefthander, Bob Hendley, duelled with uncanny perfection. Neither pitcher had allowed a hit, but in the fifth the Dodgers scored an unearned run without benefit of a hit. The first hit of the game finally came in the seventh, when the Dodgers' Lou Johnson sliced a double to right field. As Koufax went to the mound to hurl the eighth, the crowd buzzed nervously. They cheered on every pitch. The tension and excitement of 29,139 fans spilled down on the field, where Koufax prepared to pitch to Ron Santo. He looked at a third strike and the crowd roared. Ernie Banks swung and missed for a third strike and the crowd roared. Byron Browne did the same and the crowd roared again. Chris Krug, the first Cub batter in the ninth inning, struck out swinging. Koufax pitched to

pinch hitter Joey Amalfitano, who swung at three pitches
and missed them all. And then it was Harvey Kuenn, the
last batter between Koufax and a no-hitter. Three pitches,
three strikes, and Sandy Koufax had done what no other
pitcher in the annals of baseball had done—he had pitched
his fourth no-hitter and he made it a special one: He made
this one a perfect game.

"Sometimes," said Amalfitano, "you get the feeling he
can pitch a no-hitter anytime he wants to."

"When Sandy's right," his teammate Don Drysdale
said, "I'm surprised when he doesn't strike everybody out.
It wouldn't surprise me if he pitched a no-hitter every time
he went out there."

Arthritis and pain and swelling could not stop Koufax
in 1965. He did not miss a starting assignment that entire
season. He pitched 336 innings, more than any other
pitcher, and he set a strikeout record by mowing down 382
batters. He won 26 games and lost only 8, and he led the
league with a 2.04 ERA. In the World Series against the
Minnesota Twins, he came back twice to pitch with just two
days' rest. The first time found the Series tied two games
apiece, and Koufax put the Dodgers ahead with a 7–0 shutout. The second time, he came back with the Series tied
three games apiece, and he won it all for the Dodgers with
a 2–0 victory. Once again he won the Cy Young Award;
once again he was the National League's Most Valuable
Player; once again he was America's idol.

The spring of 1966 was marred by a contract dispute
with the Dodger front office, but they reached an agreement
and Koufax joined the team ten days before the start of the
season. There was much to do in a short time, so Sandy

rolled up his sleeves, took a cortisone shot and went to
work.

Again it was a brilliant season for the incomparable
left-hander. Again, by some miracle, he pitched around the
pain and the swelling and did not miss a starting assignment. He won 27 games and lost 9, struck out 317 batters
and had an ERA of 1.73. He was the Cy Young Award winner a third time. But by midseason it became obvious to
him that he could not go on like this much longer. His left
arm was so bent that he could not straighten it completely.
Things dropped out of his left hand, and the shots and medication were coming more frequently, too frequently for
Sandy's good. Six weeks before the end of the season he
made up his mind. He would pitch no more; 1966 would be
his last year.

"There's no cure and it isn't getting any better," he
confided to friends. "I can't throw the curve the way I used
to. It hurts and it's going to continue to hurt. It won't improve, and I don't want to spend the rest of my life a
cripple."

Six weeks before the end of the season he decided to
retire, but he did not quit. He could have, right there, but
he did not. He continued to pitch, and when it came down to
the last day of the season and the Dodgers needed a victory,
Sandy Koufax took the ball and went out and pitched. The
Dodgers had lost the first game of a doubleheader to Philadelphia that Sunday, October 2, 1966, and, in Pittsburgh,
the Giants defeated the Pirates. A Dodger defeat would
throw the National League pennant race into a tie, forcing a
play-off. And history told the story of how the Dodgers
made out in play-offs with the Giants.

Koufax was working with only two days' rest, working against his normal routine, working on a day he should have been resting, risking permanent injury. But he held the Phillies scoreless for eight innings as the Dodgers piled up a 6–0 lead. In the bottom of the ninth, the Phillies got a walk, an error, two singles and a double. They had three runs in, nobody out and the tying run coming to bat as Dodger manager Walter Alston walked slowly, thoughtfully to the mound. Was this a spot for a fresh pitcher? No, this was a spot for Sandy Koufax.

He got the next two batters out. The last batter was Jackie Brandt, and Sandy Koufax struck him out. He won the game and he won the pennant for the Dodgers, just as he had always done.

The wonder is not that he pitched two years with arthritis in his left elbow. The wonder is not that he pitched 54 complete games and 659 innings with an arm shot full of cortisone. The wonder is not that he struck out 699 batters and had 16 shutouts despite terrible pain and swelling. The wonder is what he might have done with a healthy arm.

And so, on December 18, 1966, six weeks before his 31st birthday, Sandy Koufax walked into the San Souci room of the Beverly-Wilshire Hotel in Beverly Hills, California. He sat at the table behind the fifteen microphones and made the solemn speech that everyone expected to hear, yet hoped they would not hear. And as you looked at the handsome face, the strong, youthful, athlete's body, you sadly asked yourself why it had to be like this. Why did the great ones have to go long before their time?

KEN VENTURI

"Hold your head up, Ken. You're a champion now."

It was 1960 and the world was a big, red, juicy apple that belonged to Ken Venturi. Lucky Ken Venturi. Here was a guy who had everything. He had just won the Milwaukee Open golf tournament—they handed him a check for $4,300 and lucky Ken Venturi put his clubs in his bag and headed home.

In two days it would be September. It had been a long, tiresome year on the professional golfers' tour. A successful year. His purses totalled $41,230, which was enough for him. He would take the rest of the year off and rest up for the grind that would begin all over again in January. Back in Hillsborough, California, a suburb of San Francisco, a lovely new home awaited him. So did his wife, Conni, who was beautiful enough to be a movie star, and two fine sons, Matthew and Tim.

There was no bigger name in golf in 1960 than Ken Venturi. Only Arnold Palmer earned more money in purses, but Ken was comparatively new on the tour and getting better every year. Young boys idolized him and old men envied him. His closest friends were some of the most famous people in the field of entertainment. And he had put behind him a reputation as an egotist and a sorehead that, at one time, made him one of the most unpopular players on the tour. Venturi had matured and, at 29, was at the top of his game. The future was bright, and anyone who followed the wonderful world of golf was not surprised at the progress Ken had made in his four years as a professional.

Ken had practically been raised on a golf course. His father ran the pro shop at San Francisco's Harding Park Municipal golf course, and almost from the time he could walk, Ken was swinging a club. When he was thirteen, Ken watched Byron Nelson demolish Ben Hogan by nineteen strokes in the San Francisco Open. The boy was so impressed that he began to emulate Nelson's style. So it was a big day in young Venturi's life when arrangements were made for him to meet and play a round with the great master.

Venturi shot a 66 and, full of himself, said to Nelson, "How was that?"

"Meet me at the first tee tomorrow morning at 9," was Nelson's answer. "There are six or seven things wrong with your game that need fixing."

The two met often on the golf course after that. Nelson corrected little flaws in Venturi's game and watched the young man improve steadily. Old-timers who saw Venturi were astonished. Watching him was like watching a young Byron Nelson.

By the time he was 17, Ken was competing in national junior championships. At 21 he won the San Francisco city championship and played in the America's Cup in Seattle against Canada and Mexico. The following year he was a member of the United States Walker Cup team that defeated England in Marion, Massachusetts. His game was improving, his reputation was growing, and Venturi was being hailed as one of the top amateurs in the country and a pro star of the future.

Ken's progress was temporarily curtailed when he was drafted by the Army in 1954. For two years he did not touch a club, but when he was discharged in 1956, it did not take him long to regain the touch and his high amateur standing. He was so highly regarded that he was invited to play in the 1956 Masters Tournament at Augusta, Georgia, as an amateur.

He was just 24 and playing with the big boys, but Venturi did not fall apart at the opportunity. He shot a 66 on the first day, and when all the scores were in, he startled the golf world by leading a field that included the biggest names in the game. No amateur had ever shot a 66 in the

Masters, and no amateur had ever led the field after the first three rounds. When they started the final eighteen holes, Ken Venturi held a remarkable four-shot edge over Dr. Cary Middlecoff. By holding any part of that advantage, Ken Venturi would make golfing history: he would be the first amateur to win the coveted Masters coat.

It has long been a Masters tradition that Byron Nelson pair off for the final round with the tournament leader. However, aware of the close relationship between Nelson and Venturi and hoping to avoid criticism that Venturi was coached through the last eighteen holes, the directors of the tournament moved Venturi's starting time back two hours and paired him with Sam Snead, the hardened old pro. Angered by the switch, awed by his closeness to victory, anxious to show up the tournament directors and aware of Middlecoff at his heels, Venturi blew up and shot an amateurish 80 on the final round. Ironically, he managed to hold off Middlecoff, but Jackie Burke, who had started the round eight strokes back, shot a 71 to beat Ken by one stroke.

Venturi was so disappointed and disillusioned that he could not control his anger. He lashed out at the directors of the tournament, charging they had conspired to beat him out of the title because he was an amateur.

The story of an amateur's blast at the old and time-honored Masters was picked up by the press and spread all over the country, to the embarrassment of Venturi. Repentant, he sent a 184-word telegram to Bobby Jones, president of the Augusta National Golf Course, and to Cliff Roberts, tournament director, in which he apologized for his remarks. Some statements, he said, were misunderstood while others were made impulsively and he regretted them. Jones and Roberts accepted the apology, saying the telegram represented a "splendid and courageous effort." Venturi, they said, would be welcome at the 1957 Masters.

Jones and Roberts might have been willing to forgive and forget, but Venturi was not exactly greeted with open arms by his new colleagues when he turned pro on November 29, 1956. He was considered a sorehead and a crybaby. Ken Venturi is not like that, but reputations die slowly among athletes, and it took Ken years to erase his.

Venturi made his professional debut in the Bing Crosby tournament on January 9, 1957. Seven months later he had his first tour victory, winning the St. Paul Open with a record-tying 266 and collecting $2,800. The following week he won the Milwaukee Open and $6,000. Now he was moving. He was being hailed as the next of the great golfers and his smooth, picture swing was being compared with Ben Hogan's. No tournament was complete without Venturi's entry, and when he went home in 1960, he had won ten championships and pocketed $157,000 in official purses on the PGA tour. He also had more than twice that much in endorsements and appearances. Ken Venturi was on his way. Lucky Ken Venturi.

Success could not spoil Ken Venturi. Neither could it make him complacent. He was so close to being the top player on the tour he could taste it, and it tasted sweet. He wanted it. He knew he was going to have to compete with Palmer and therefore would have to get more distance on his drives. He altered his swing ever so slightly, hoping to attain extra power. Instead it had a reverse effect. Suddenly he could do nothing right. When he should have been getting better, winning more, his game was going backward. He did not fall apart completely—Ken was too good a golfer for that. He managed to win $25,572 in 1961, but he went through the entire season without winning a tournament. Veterans on the tour began to wonder what had happened to the promising young star.

His swing was disrupted, he lost his groove and, it seemed, his confidence was shaken. Venturi began to panic. He blew important shots that cost him valuable strokes and thousands of dollars. He was overcome by fear as he tried to check the slide, repair his game and regain the touch that had made him one of golf's brightest young stars.

Then it was January 1962 at the Palm Springs Classic. He three-putted the tenth hole and, as he bent over to pick the ball out of the cup, it hit him . . . a sharp, searing pain in his chest. He thought it was his heart, but doctors could find nothing organically wrong with him. There was no reason, they said, why he could not continue to play golf and play it well. But when he tried to play the pain returned, and his once flawless form did not. He could not lift his right hand to comb his hair, and when he swung a golf club, pain flashed through his right side. He tried everything. Cortisone, whirlpool baths, deep heat treatments. Nothing worked. When the 1962 season ended, Venturi had earned only $6,951.39 in 27 tournaments.

It was worse in 1963. His earnings for the year tumbled to $3,848.33. He was tormented by bad golf and by pain, real or imagined, and all the skills he once possessed had vanished mysteriously, inexplicably. Now the whole thing was getting away from him. He regained a stammer in his speech which he had had as a boy, and a muscle in his chin began twitching nervously. Things were so bad he considered quitting the game. Endorsement contracts he had signed in the good days were not renewed, and a golf equipment company in which he had invested went bankrupt. He was broke and almost broken.

"I just lost confidence in myself," he says. "I became so discouraged."

He began to see a hypnotist but that did not help. Then he started to pay frequent visits to a family friend, Father Francis Kevin Murray of the St. Vincent DePaul Church in San Francisco.

"Father Murray was the only person I could talk to," Ken explains. "The only person I could tell my troubles to outside of my family."

Father Murray tried to restore Ken's confidence, his faith in himself. With his help, Venturi tried to pull himself together for one last tour. He went to Byron Nelson for help with his game, just as he had gone to Father Murray for help with his spirit. He had enough money left to finance one more year on the tour. He would give it a try. If he failed, he would put his clubs away forever and look for another way of making a living.

Once he was one of the big names. Right up there with the Palmers and Players and Sneads. You did not run a major golf tournament without inviting Ken Venturi, even if he was a bit egocentric. He was a big name and he had a following, and to exclude him would be to invite criticism and contempt for your tournament. But when he started playing poorly, it was easy not to invite him. More and more frequently, Ken found himself on the outside looking in, too proud to ask for an invitation. His reputation was

coming back to haunt him. They did not dare snub him
when he was going well, but now they didn't need him. Let
him suffer. Nobody sympathized with Ken Venturi.

He made his first start of 1964 on January 3 in the
Los Angeles Open and failed to make the cut. He failed to
make the cut in the Bing Crosby tournament and in the
Palm Springs Classic, but he did not quit. In March he
played in the Pensacola Open and won $1,100, his first
four-figure check in two years. Two weeks later he picked
up $950 at Doral. It was not a fortune, but it was a start.

He arrived at the registration desk of one tournament
only to be told he had not been invited and to be turned
away. But the unkindest cut came when he failed to receive
an invitation to play in the Masters. He thought he would
always be invited to the Masters. Just eight years ago he
almost made history when he failed by one stroke to become
the first amateur to win the tournament; and just four years
ago, as a young pro, he was again beaten by one stroke,
this time by Arnold Palmer. He watched the 1964 Masters
tournament on television at home, and he longed to be out
there on the golf course.

Then it was June and the tour was moving to the big
Thunderbird Classic in New York. The Thunderbird was a
rich tournament and one which carried a great deal of
prestige. Venturi wanted to play in it for the exposure and
because he could feel the touch returning. He thought he
could do well. Heaven knows, he needed the money desperately. He waited for his invitation but it did not come,
and so he said to himself, "All right, if they want me to get
on my hands and knees and beg, that's what I'll do."

He picked up the telephone and invested in a long
distance call to New York. Tournament directors were hesi-

tant, so Ken begged. They didn't know . . . and he begged some more. Well, there was one spot open, but they were saving it for a last-minute entry . . . and Ken pleaded. "Okay," they said, "you're in, Ken Venturi."

He packed his bags and headed for New York. He finished in a third place tie. As soon as he had holed out, he made a mad dash for the nearest telephone. "Conni," he almost shouted into the phone. "Honey, we're back in business. We won $6,250." And for two minutes, the two of them sobbed and wept long distance. Ken Venturi was on the way back.

In a month they would be playing the big one, the United States Open in Washington, D.C., and Venturi packed his bags and headed south. It was crazy, it was senseless, it was far-fetched, but he packed his bags anyway. It was hot and humid in the nation's Capital that June, and the Congressional Country Club course was a monstrous 7,053 yards, the longest in Open history. It had been four years since Venturi played in the Open and four years since he won a tournament, but he was filled with a new spirit, a new confidence.

It was 84 degrees and muggy that first day. Ken shot a 72, which left him four shots behind Palmer. On the second day Venturi had a respectable 70 to Palmer's 69, but Tommy Jacobs came in with a brilliant 64. On the third day they were to play 36 holes. The sun came up early and it came up hot. Everyone knew it would be a scorcher of a day, and Ken was grateful for the early tee-off time he had been assigned. He could get his first eighteen holes in before the midday sun had taken its full effect.

He knew there was slim chance of overtaking the leader, Tommy Jacobs, who had a six-stroke edge on him, or overtaking the runner-up, Palmer, who was one stroke behind Jacobs. But Ken felt he was in a good position to finish high on the money list if he had another good day.

Then, on the first green, something happened that changed it all for Ken Venturi. Something happened that made him think only of winning. It was impossible, but he thought about it anyway. He stuck his approach shot ten feet from the pin. His putt for a birdie was straight and true but not strong enough, as it came to rest on the lip of the cup. Veterans in the gallery expected Venturi to gnash his teeth, throw his club, curse his luck as he might have done just a few years ago. But this was a new Ken Venturi.

"Wait a while," he calmly told his playing partner, Raymond Floyd, "it will fall. They always do."

They waited a full minute, then the ball dropped into the cup as if by some mystical force. From then on there was no stopping him. He made a 25-footer on eight and curled in a 10-footer on nine. He made the turn in thirty, and as he walked to the tenth tee, someone told him he had pulled into a tie with Jacobs.

But there were still 27 holes to go. The sun had come up stronger and Venturi could feel the heat sapping the strength from his body. He had been too nervous to eat breakfast and he had hardly any energy left. He always had been a very slow player, but now he was practically crawling around the course. He managed to keep pace with Jacobs through sixteen, but on the seventeenth it hit him. He began to get chills and hot flashes, his stomach ached from cramps and he felt nauseous. But he was determined to finish. He dragged himself through the last two holes of the morning round, with eighteen still to go in the afternoon. He bogied the seventeenth. He bogied the eighteenth and it looked like he was through.

He finished with a 66, but he gave Tommy Jacobs a breather. He had made a gallant run at the leader, but now was two shots back, he was sick and tired, and there was serious doubt that he could *start* the final eighteen, let alone finish.

In the gallery was Dr. John Everett, a Congressional Club member. He followed Venturi into the clubhouse and began ministering to him. Ken had 45 minutes before he must go out into the blast furnace again. Dr. Everett had Venturi lie down and he fed him tea and salt tablets, one after another.

"Hey, Doc," Ken mumbled, "whose side are you on?"

Now it was time to go out for the last eighteen holes. Ken felt he could not make it, but he knew he would try. He had many reasons to try, and one of them was contained in a letter he carried in his pocket. He had received it just that morning. It said:

> Dear Ken. For you to become the 1964 USA Open champion would be one of the greatest things that can possibly happen in our country this year. Should you win, the effect would be both a blessing and a tonic to so many people who desperately need encouragement and a reason for hope. Most people are in the midst of unremitting struggle involving their jobs, their family problems, their health, frustrations of various sorts, even the insecurity of life itself. For many there is a pressing temptation to give up, to quit trying. Life at times simply seems to be too much, its demands overpowering.
>
> If you should win, Ken, you would prove, I believe, to millions everywhere that they, too, can be victorious over doubt, misfortune and despair. I'll be here with your mother and father and the children watching you on TV. . . .
>
> Your friend, Father Murray.

It was 2:30 and the temperature had soared over 100 when Ken appeared at the first tee, the familiar white, peaked cap glinting in the bright sun. With him was Dr. Everett, carrying a wet towel wrapped around a plastic bag filled with ice. Also there was Joe Dey, executive director of the USGA.

Venturi played magnificently, almost mechanically. He seemed to be playing on instinct and guts alone. He recovered from a bunker and parred the par three second hole to draw even with Jacobs. Venturi parred the first five holes, bogied the sixth, then birdied the ninth. He was two shots ahead as he made the turn.

Congressional had become an inferno. On the last nine holes exhaustion took over and Venturi was playing as if from memory. His slow, Stan Laurel-like walk became slower, his body dragged, he seemed hardly able to put one foot in front of the other, he labored on each shot. He birdied the thirteenth and was ahead by four strokes. He had nobody to beat but the heat and his own fatigue.

At fourteen an official held a thermometer showing 112 degrees. Venturi's pace became agonizingly slow. His face was ashen, his gaze trance-like. He hit his tee shot on seventeen and, as he crawled up the fairway, he turned to Joe Dey and said, "You can penalize me two shots for slow play, but I've just got to walk slowly." He sat on his bag waiting to putt on the seventeenth green, and he appeared emotionally and physically spent. At eighteen he was on the green in two. As he struggled down the fairway into a sea of faces rimming the green, he heard Joe Dey speak.

"Hold your head up, Ken," he said. "You're a champion now."

Venturi rests before trudging up the final fairway in his National Open victory.

The people were applauding and the sound of it was good. It gave him strength to line up his ten-foot putt. Now there was a hushed silence as he leaned over the ball and gently tapped it into the cup. It was finished. Ken Venturi had made it. He was the United States Open champion! Like a man in a daze, Venturi took his white cap in his hand and waved it in gratitude to the cheering crowd.

Slowly, painfully, he walked to the official scoring table and sat down heavily, gratefully, the cheers still ringing in his ears. He pushed his cap to the top of his head and he buried his face in his hands. He sat that way for what seemed an eternity. Finally, when he picked his head up, there were tears streaming down his cheeks.

Ken Venturi had come back. The check for winning the Open was $17,000 and it did not stop there. He parlayed his victory into five times that amount in endorsements and appearances. And to prove it was no fluke, he won first money in the Insurance City Open and the American Golf Classic, and picked up sizable checks in the St. Paul Open and the Whitemarsh Open.

It was like old times once again. Ken Venturi was a hero. Endorsements came pouring in. There were banquets, speeches, awards and hardly enough time to fulfill all the commitments. Ken Venturi was wanted again. Everybody wanted him to play in their tournament and now he could be selective; now he could be particular. Invitations came from all over the world, and he chose his spots carefully.

In October he accepted an invitation to play at Wentworth, England. When he arrived he was hailed as a champion, greeted as a hero, idolized as a man who had overcome hardships with remarkable courage and perserverance.

But almost as suddenly as it came, it all began to slip away from him again. It was cold and rainy at Wentworth and Ken noticed the tips of his fingers begin to peel. He dismissed it, blaming it on the weather. But several weeks later in Mexico, his fingers grew numb and puffy. His weight suddenly and inexplicably began to tumble. He went from 173 to 160. His cheeks began to puff and his fingers swelled with fluid. Some days there would be no feeling in his hands, and other days there would be agonizing pain.

It got so that Ken prayed for the pain because he could tolerate that much more than the numbness.

"When my hands are numb," he explained, "I can hit the ball far, but I don't hit it straight because there is no feeling. When I have feeling, I do not hit it far, but at least I hit straight."

Against the advice of doctors he played the Bing Crosby Open in January 1965. He had to find out if he could still play. He could not. Using hand warmers between shots, he had rounds of 81, 75 and 77 and failed to qualify for the final.

He went to the famous Mayo Clinic in Rochester, Minnesota, where doctors tried everything. They said he had Raynaud's Phenomenon, the same rare circulatory problem that had earlier struck Sandy Koufax. The doctors did all they could to correct it. They cut into his left side and his left shinbone; they fed him cortisone and other drugs and had him dip his hands in hot paraffin solution to encourage circulation. None of the remedies worked. Would he consent to another operation? This time they would cut into his wrists to relieve the blockage.

Ken agreed, but first he had to do something. He had to defend his United States Open championship. It was a promise he made when he won at Congressional. He would go as far as he could.

"I will play if they have to carry me around in a basket," he said. "I may have to hockey it around, but I have no intention of withdrawing."

He picked up his clubs again and began preparing for the Open. Sometimes he played without feeling and other times with excruciating pain. He began a daily routine designed to restore the circulation in his hands just long enough to get through a round of golf.

He would start each day by massaging his numb and swollen hands to get the circulation going. At the same time his wife massaged his back. After two hours, he would stand under a hot shower for half an hour to get the blood flowing in his fingers. Then he would be ready to start his day on the golf course.

He went to the Bellerive Country Club in St. Louis to play in the 1965 United States Open, but he did not play well. It was embarrassing and humiliating.

"I felt awful for him," said Gene Littler, who played in the threesome with Venturi and Billy Campbell. "It was terrible. He couldn't even hit the ball out of his own shadow."

"It was a heart-breaking thing," Campbell said. "He was in great pain, you could tell. But he didn't complain. Not once."

The pain was unbearable, but he had made a promise so he did not complain and he did not quit. He struggled through and shot an 81 the first day and a 79 the second day. He failed to make the cut, but he did not quit until he had played the minimum 36 holes. Others quit, but Ken Venturi played until he was formally eliminated. It hurt him to play, but he finished like a champion, dropping a 35-foot putt on his last hole. Then he packed his bags and went to the Mayo Clinic. He did not know if he would ever play golf again, but there were no complaints, no regrets.

"I thank God," he said, "for the last twelve months. At least I had that. It was a great thrill. It was something I had worked 34 years for. I don't know exactly how to describe it, but maybe this will explain it. I wrote a book of my life story and there are two chapters devoted to the 1964 Open. It took me thirty hours to write those two chapters . . . to express what I felt. Thirty hours to get it just right."

They operated on him in the Mayo Clinic. Large medical terms were used to explain just what they did, and even Ken Venturi did not understand it all. In simple terms, they made two-inch cuts on both hands between the thumb and the wrist to remove the blockage and let the blood circulate freely into his fingers. An hour after the operation, he was on the telephone talking to a friend: "I'll be all right," he promised. "I'll play golf again, you'll see."

Now it was the start of the 1966 season and Ken entered the Los Angeles Open. Again it was against doctors' wishes, but he had to find out. He had to know if he could play golf again. He had earned $295 in all of 1965. In the good days, Venturi handed out more than $295 in tips.

He was starting his second comeback at the age of 35. He finished eighth in Los Angeles and won $637.50. The numbness and pain were almost gone and he could feel the touch returning. But he was not doing any celebrating as the tour moved to San Francisco, his home town, to the Harding Park Municipal course where he played so often as a boy and where his father still operated the pro shop.

He played well the first three rounds, and he entered the final nine holes four strokes behind the leader, Frank Beard. Beard faltered on the back nine and Ken Venturi, who would not quit when the odds against him were so overwhelming, played steady golf to draw even. Then, on the sixteenth, he sank a ten-foot birdie putt and he was ahead to stay.

For the second time he had come back. He won the $8,500 first prize money and, more important than that, he won the championship. He was champion of the 1966 Lucky Invitational golf tournament.

He was lucky Ken Venturi.

JIM RYUN

"The name of the game is pain."

A letter in the files of Bob Timmons, varsity track and field coach at the University of Kansas, is among his most prized possessions. It was not sent by the President of the United States or by some great athlete, past or present. It was sent by a high school track coach, a rival of Timmons' when he coached at Wichita East High School. The letter is a testamonial to the benefits of hard work and training; it disputes the ancient belief that great athletes are born, not made; it is proof that a man can attain anything he wants if he wants it badly enough, if he is willing to sacrifice and work hard enough to achieve it.

The letter was written in the fall of 1962, a few days after Timmons had taken a "B" squad to Kansas City and won the team championship in a cross-country meet of such little significance that it did not rate so much as a line in the local papers. When Timmons returned to Wichita the letter was waiting on his desk. "Dear coach," it said, "Congratulations on your team's victory. It was quite an achievement, particularly since there are no outstanding runners on your squad."

It was meant as sincere praise from one coach to another because, in fact, there was nobody on the Wichita East team who really caught your eye. It had been a victory attributable to excellent coaching and team balance. The first Wichita runner across the finish line had been a tall, gangly kid who finished sixth.

Less than two years later, that tall, gangly kid had broken the four-minute mile. Two years after that he was the world record holder for the mile.

But that high school coach from Kansas City is not to be condemned as a poor judge of talent. Very few people foresaw the spark of greatness that was in Jim Ryun; very few detected the spark of determination that was housed within him; and nobody could know of the hard work and sacrifice that would be necessary to bring out that greatness and determination.

There is a stubbornness and a seeming resistance to pain that characterizes Jim Ryun. Once, when he was very young, Jim got a stomachache, but told no one about it until the pain became so severe he thought his stomach would burst. Jim's mother rushed him to the hospital with not a minute to spare. His appendix had burst, and in only a matter of minutes he would have died from peritonitis, rupture of the abdominal membrane.

Although he probably never would have grown up to be a robust lad anyway, the illness left Jim skinny and frail and too weak to compete in most sports. Baseball had always been his first love, but he went out for the track team as a quarter-miler at Curtiss Junior High in Wichita, Kansas. He ran a 58.5 and was told by the coach to forget track and find another sport. Jim did. He concentrated his athletic activity on a once-a-week bowling league.

Jim Ryun might never have had another chance to run if it were not for coach Bob Timmons, a very persuasive man for all of his five feet, three and one-half inch height. Jim had moved on to Wichita East High where he heard coach Timmons make an impassioned plea for cross-country runners. At least one sophomore was moved by the talk, and that afternoon Jim Ryun showed up on the track with a handful of cross-country candidates.

Timmons put the group through a series of time trials. Ryun ran a 54-second 440, 2:22 for the half-mile, 5:28 for the mile and 11:51 for the two-mile, hardly the kind of times that would leave a lasting impression or indicate any hope for the future.

"I didn't even know how to spell his last name," Timmons admits. "I kept spelling it R-Y-A-N."

But there was something about the boy that appealed to Timmons. Something told him, instinctively, that here was a boy who might be worth working with and developing. What Timmons saw in Ryun was a lean, hungry look and a graceful, long-legged gait. But mostly, he seemed to possess a desire to succeed and a willingness to work hard and sacrifice to achieve success, qualities which are extremely rare in one so young.

Under Timmons' guidance, Ryun began a training program that was to become a regular routine and a part of his life all through high school. He arose each morning at 4:30, delivered the papers on his newspaper route and then ran six miles before breakfast. After school he would run six more miles before supper.

It is necessary to suffer to achieve greatness in something like distance running, which gives no bonus points for the natural gifts of speed and strength. It is an endurance game, and endurance is rewarded only to those who are willing to pay the price, to work hard, to suffer. It takes a special kind of willpower. To some it might mean passing up a piece of strawberry shortcake, and to others it might mean getting out and running instead of passing the time with the gang at the local hangout. Jim Ryun has the kind of willpower and dedication that made him get out and run. It was not easy. "Most of the time while I was running in the mornings," he says, "I thought about how nice it would be to be back in my nice warm bed."

The climate in Kansas varies from ice, deep snow and blizzards in the winter to 100-degree heat under a blazing sun in the summer. Through it all, Ryun ran. Every day, twice a day, hot or cold, rainy or sunny, he ran.

"The name of the game," says J. D. Edmiston, Timmons' successor at Wichita East when Timmons moved on to Kansas in Ryun's senior year, "is pain. And Jim can take it with the best of them."

In his extreme modesty, Ryun minimizes his suffering and his sacrifices. "I think too much is made of the pain stuff," he says. "Running doesn't hurt that much. I've often tried to explain to people that there is more satisfaction than pain in a hard workout, but I guess too many of them can't understand that work can be satisfying. Besides, if running a race hurt as much as people seem to think it does, I wouldn't get out on the track in the first place."

Only Jim Ryun can know the pain he has felt, and only Jim Ryun can know the satisfaction he has felt. What he is really saying is that satisfaction makes the pain worthwhile. But he has suffered. He has suffered with an allergy that makes breathing difficult when he runs. His throat gets rough and raw and he often finishes a race coughing and sick with exhaustion. He must have his throat scraped periodically, and each week he must get an allergy shot. He has suffered, too, from defective hearing, the result of inner-ear damage following a childhood virus. This often leaves him with the disadvantage of not being able to hear his quarter times when he is chasing a record and the crowd is screaming.

What makes Jim run despite these handicaps is a desire for success, a hunger to be the best at whatever he does and a knowledge that nothing worthwhile comes easily. Jim Ryun is that kind of young man.

"He didn't run into track," says his mother, "he dived into it. In the ninth grade he couldn't make the team and

the coach said he'd never make a runner. Yet in the next
year he came in second in his first high school mile, and he
won every high school mile he was in after that. But I was
always concerned that he was going to hurt himself physically. I thought he would ruin his health. When he'd come
home at night he'd be sick and too tired to eat his dinner.
He'd throw up after every race. He'd go to bed without
eating his food night after night."

This, too, is the kind of young man Jim Ryun is. "At
first, he'd always try too hard, before he had enough
strength," says his dad, a toolmaker at an aircraft factory
in Wichita. "He had vision, I guess, but his body wasn't
trained. He'd tear off and pull ligaments. His body wasn't
ready, and he had to suffer to get ready."

So Jim Ryun suffered and he got ready. He got ready
to take on a whole world of runners. When a boy has that
kind of dedication, improvement comes in giant steps: in
the second competive high school mile he ever ran, he was
timed in 4:26.4. By the end of his sophomore year, all the
hard work and all the suffering were beginning to produce
their rewards. He broke the national mile record for sopho-
mores, held by Archie San Romani, Jr., and it was then
that Timmons began to get excited over the potential of his
lean, lanky sophomore. Ryun broke the record with much
less training and experience than San Romani had, and
without the benefit of a father who had once been a champion miler.

"I began talking to him about running a four-minute
mile in high school," Timmons said. "I tried to impress
upon him that a four-minute mile was possible. Since he

had so little experience, it didn't impress him so much and he wasn't scared of the barrier."

If Ryun was not scared, he was at least respectful. "At first I didn't think it could be done," he admits, "then I thought it might be possible."

It had been accepted for years among track people that the mile was a question of maturity. All the great milers did not reach their peak until the middle and late twenties. But Jim Ryun, an exploder of myths who proved great runners are made, not born, set out to explode another myth.

During his junior year Ryun kept coming closer and closer to the four-minute barrier, and Timmons knew the time was right to try for it. He had the date and the race all picked out. He entered Jim in the mile run of the Compton Relays on June 5, 1964, just six weeks after Ryun's seventeenth birthday. He would be competing against some of the world's greatest milers, and the pace was certain to be fast enough to pull Ryun along to the ultimate of his ability.

Nobody expected Ryun to win the race and he did not. He finished eighth. But his time was 3:59! He was the first high school boy to break four minutes for the mile.

Sometimes it is unfortunate that the Olympic Games, that great and remote dream of anyone who has ever laced on a pair of track shoes, should come along only every four years. For some it comes a year or two too late, past the time when they have reached their peak. For Jim Ryun, the 1964 Olympic Games at Tokyo came too early. He was good, awfully good, but he was just seventeen, a baby competing against men. A little fish in a huge pond filled with stronger, more experienced, more mature foes. There has been the hint of a suggestion that he competed with a damaged ankle in Tokyo, but that did not come from Ryun.

He ran in the second heat of the 1500-meter run and he ran well, gliding effortlessly around the track and chasing Michel Bernard of France, Jurgen May of Germany and John Whetton of Great Britain across the finish line in the good time of 3:44.4. It qualified Ryun for the semifinals, where he was pitted against Peter Snell of New Zealand and Jim Grelle of the United States. Although it was a mismatch in age and experience, Ryun stayed in the race as they came around the half-mile mark. He lay in fourth position, maintaining the blistering pace of the leaders. Then Snell made his move from behind. He moved up slowly, strongly from the back of the pack and, as if this was the spring that set each runner off, they all came alive, jostling, bumping, driving to keep up with the strong, smooth New Zealander.

At that point it all came apart for Jim Ryun. At that point he became a baby once again, getting bumped, pocketed and caught in the traffic flowing freely around him. He struggled to free himself, to get out, to find running room, but he was fighting futilely like a drowning man. He panicked and spent his energy fighting for survival, for a release from the trap of human arms and legs all around him. He dropped back and finished last in a nine-man field with a disappointing 3:55. The Olympics were all over for Jim Ryun.

There are some who will say it was for the best. To win something so big at such an early age would have de-

stroyed incentive. But nobody who really knows Jim Ryun
would believe that to be true. Complacency and satisfaction
have never been a part of his makeup.

"Ryun hates the talk of records or goals," says coach
Bob Timmons. "He regards his goals as very private
things."

And Ryun's father once said: "If we were sitting
around talking and his mother or I mentioned one of his
records, he'd scold us for bringing it up."

In a race during his sophomore year in high school,
Jim came in third, four seconds under the fastest time ever
made by a schoolboy miler. When asked how he had done,
Ryun replied, "Only third." When asked what his time had
been, he said, "It was no big deal. Third is third."

Another time he ran the fastest mile and half mile in
high school history on the same day, but lost both races to
college runners. It was an achievement to be proud of, a
reason to be excited, an opportunity to boast.

"What did you tell your folks?" asked Timmons,
enthusiastically.

"That I lost," Ryun said.

He lost in Tokyo, too, and it did not matter that it
was in the Olympic Games and that he was running against
the best in the world. He lost, he was not good enough, he
was disappointed in himself. He returned home for more
hard work, more suffering, and to wait another four years
with the fires of desire raging even more fiercely within him.

He was a high school boy again, competing against
other high school boys. On May 15, 1965, in the Kansas
State championships, he ran 3:58.3 to set a national high

school record. Three weeks later he again faced Snell and
Grelle, this time at the Compton Relays. He was eighteen
years old and had not yet graduated from high school; he
finished third behind Snell and Grelle in the fantastic time
of 3:56.8, just .4 seconds behind the leader. It was better
than he had done in Tokyo, but it was not good enough. He
had not been suffering merely to finish third. Third is third.

In the National AAU championships three weeks later,
Ryun followed a different plan against Snell. He let Snell
take the lead and he trailed him until the last quarter mile.
Then he jumped him. He shot out ahead of the Olympic
champion and sprinted to the tape, outkicking the great
Snell and beating him with a time of 3:55.3. It was the
fastest mile ever run by an American, and this American
was only eighteen years old. Where did he go from there?

Jim Ryun's next stop was the University of Kansas,
where he enrolled as a freshman and was reunited with his
old high school coach, Bob Timmons. Together they made
ambitious plans for the future and worked hard to fulfill
those plans. There appeared to be no way to stop Jim Ryun
from going right to the top, but Timmons refused to allow
Jim to relax and refused to grow complacent.

"I just worry that he'll get the idea he's arrived,"
Timmons said with typical coachly caution. "When the day
comes that he thinks he's arrived, he'll be finished. If he
doesn't continue to improve, then people are going to cut
him to ribbons. He has to give up some of the things college
kids do. If he has all the social life some youngsters have,
if he's got a girl friend and he's got a car and he's doing
all these things that some college kids do, that's fine. But

he won't be a champion runner. He has to sacrifice, the same way the kid who makes straight A's has to sacrifice. He lives a Spartan life by his own decision. I don't threaten him or force him. I feel that he ought to become the best miler in the world, but I'm an outsider and it doesn't matter how outsiders feel. It's all up to Jim. He does the work, he gets the credit and he should make the decisions about himself. He has to decide for himself if he wants to go to the top of the world."

Jim Ryun made the decision for himself, and he got to the top of the world on a sun-drenched Sunday, July 17, 1966, at Berkeley, California. It was supposed to be a dual meet between the United States and Poland, but Poland cancelled out and it was just another ordinary track meet until Jim Ryun made it something extraordinary.

The race had been scheduled at 1500 meters, the metric mile, as a concession to the Poles. But with Poland out, meet directors switched it to the mile, glamour event in American track and field. It turned out to be a fortuitous change.

Something told Jim Ryun when he arrived at Edwards Stadium on the campus of the University of California that this was going to be a very special day. Warming up he felt a surge of excitement. He was light and exuberant. He felt strong and ready for a good race.

On his mind was the world mile record of 3:53.6 set by Michel Jazy of France. Just six weeks earlier in Compton Jim had missed it by one-tenth of a second. He had been disappointed, although he had set a record for a mile on American soil. He recovered from his disappointment, and

three weeks after Compton he ran 3:58.6 at the National
AAU championships in New York. It was the first sub-four-
minute mile in the East, and it was the ninth time in his
career that Ryun had run under four minutes. He was
breaking barriers and destroying myths all over the country.

Now he waited anxiously for the starter's gun in
Berkeley. He felt so confident that he even forgot a recur-
ring soreness on the outside of his right knee that had
pained him all week. The starter fired his gun and the field
was on its way.

Tom Van Ruden set the early pace, passing the first
quarter in 57.7. When Wade Bell led at the half in 1:55.4,
Ryun knew the pace was right for a shot at the world record.
He was running third, and just after he heard the time for
the half, he moved up to second place behind Bell, preparing for his big move. With 700 yards to go, Jim stepped
out and bolted into the lead as if shot out of a cannon. He
was on his way and the fans sensed it. All 15,000 of them
were on their feet cheering the young man on.

The three-quarter time was announced . . . 2:55.3. The
stadium exploded with cheers and applause, and buzzed
with the anticipation of history being made before their
eyes. Ryun was a galloping stallion now, running smoothly
and powerfully, picking up momentum and speed, racing
against the clock as he approached the world record and
the finish line, both of which were only a few breaths away.
He burst through the tape with a fury and he knew he had
broken the world record. The crowd knew it too, for they
were on their feet cheering wildly as Jim Ryun slowed his
pace imperceptibly to lope once more around the track,

waving gratefully to acknowledge the shower of adulation pouring down upon him from the stands.

They were still cheering when the official time was announced—3:51.3, breaking the world record by 2.3 seconds. He was the first American to hold the cherished mile record since Glenn Cunningham, another Kansan, held it 29 years earlier.

They swarmed around him, officials, fellow athletes and newspapermen, and in his joy, Jim Ryun hardly thought about the throbbing pain in his right knee.

"It is the most beautiful pain I have ever had," he said.

He had his world record, but it was not the end for Jim Ryun. Ahead of him was Mexico City and the Olympic Games in 1968. Ahead of him was much more pain and much more hard work and much more self-sacrifice, all of which he knows he must endure until he has achieved the ultimate of his goals—the Olympic championship.

MAURY WILLS

"Go on back home and forget major league baseball. You're just too little, kid."

Maury Wills remembers the day as if it were yesterday, but, really, it was many yesterdays ago. It was the spring of 1959 to be exact, on a clear, warm, bright morning in Lakeland, Florida, the spring training camp of the Detroit Tigers.

In two days the Tigers would break camp and head north. Maury Wills felt certain he would be with them, and the thought filled him with a feeling of anticipation and excitement. He had never played in a major league game, and he had marked the date well. April 10, 1959. The Tigers would open the season in Detroit that day against the Chicago White Sox. Maury imagined himself in the white uniform with the navy blue, old English "D" over his heart and the number 37 on his back, waiting at shortstop for the first pitch of the season.

He was 26 years old and he had played professional baseball for eight years, but he had never even been in a major league training camp before. All of those eight years were spent in the Dodger organization. Each spring he would go to their huge training quarters, a renovated Army barracks at Vero Beach, Florida, and always he would be tossed in with the minor league players. He lived with the minor leaguers, dressed with the minor leaguers, worked with the minor leaguers and ate with the minor leaguers.

In Vero Beach Wills was just another shortstop. The Dodgers had the veteran Pee Wee Reese at the position and a list of prospects as long as the guest list at a Perle Mesta party. There was Don Zimmer and Charlie Neal, Chico Fernandez and Bob Lillis, Charlie Smith and Bob Aspromonte and dozens more ambitious young fellows scampering around the camp. Wills could run and field with any of them, but the word on him was that he could not hit and he was too small for major league ball.

After the 1958 season the Tigers, desperate for help at shortstop, inquired about Wills. The Dodgers, not particularly anxious to hold him, arranged a deal. Maury would report to Lakeland the following spring to work with the Tigers. If they liked him, they would pay the Dodgers $35,000 for his contract. If not, Maury would be returned.

For the first time Wills felt like a big leaguer, because for the first time he was treated like one. He worked with the big leaguers and he lived and ate with them. He was assigned a locker in the big league clubhouse and he dressed alongside Al Kaline, Harvey Kuenn, Charlie Maxwell, Frank Lary and Jim Bunning.

Maury worked hard that spring, harder than he had ever worked before. He showed up at the ballpark two hours before everyone else arrived and he stayed two hours after everyone else had gone home. He worked to improve his hitting. He hit until his hands were red and raw with painful blisters, then he put on gloves and hit some more. He could feel himself getting better and he proved it whenever he got a chance to play in exhibition games. He got 11 hits in 23 times at bat, stole eight consecutive bases and did not make an error all spring. He knew he had it made in that last week when coach Billy Hitchcock began to show more interest in him, and for the first time he was getting personal attention. Hitchcock worked with him on pivoting for the double play, talked to him about how to play hitters and passed along inside information on American Leaguers that could only mean the Tigers had decided to keep him as their regular shortstop.

Thus when Wills was summoned to the office of Jim Campbell, a club vice-president, he guessed the purpose was to sign his Tiger contract and make the deal official. But Campbell had news of a different kind. "I'm sorry,

Maury," Campbell said. "We're sending you back to the Dodgers. We've decided to go along with Rocky Bridges at shortstop and we've got Coot Veal to back him up."

At first Wills was stunned. Why? he asked himself. What had he done wrong? Didn't he prove he could do the job? But somehow Maury Wills always knew this was the way he would end up, falling just short of the top. He knew it ever since that first day when he showed up at a major league tryout camp and the first baseball scout who ever talked to him said: "Go on back home and forget major league baseball. You're just too little, kid."

Maurice Morning Wills was one of thirteen children born to the wife of Guy O. Wills, a Baptist minister in Washington, D.C. In addition to his ministerial duties, Maury's dad worked full time as a government machinist in a Navy yard. And in addition to her duties as wife and mother of thirteen, Maury's mom ran an elevator in a government building.

The children were always well provided for, and Maury and his four brothers grew up with an avid interest in sports. At Cardozo High School in Washington Maury starred in football, basketball and baseball. He was only 5′8″, 150 pounds, but in football he was the T-formation quarterback and safety man and the unofficial coach of the team. "When we shifted into the single wing, I put myself at tailback," he recalls.

He could have gone to any one of nine colleges on a football scholarship, but Maury loved baseball best. He had gained a measure of prominence as a pitcher at Cardozo, but there were no professional offers when he graduated, so he went over to Griffith Stadium to a tryout camp run annually by the *Washington Daily News*. There were more than 300 boys at the camp, and representatives of every big league team were there to look over the talent. Maury took a seat in the stands and waited as instructed. After two hours Wills' still had not been called. He decided to take matters into his own hands. He climbed down from the stands and asked for his chance.

"What position do you play?" asked the man in charge.

"I'm a pitcher."

"A pitcher? A little guy like you? All right, warm up, you pitch next."

He pitched two innings, striking out all six men he faced, and was disappointed when all he got for his effort was an invitation to come back the next day for another look. He did. The next day he faced three men and again struck them all out. For this, he was invited to a three-day tryout in Havre de Grace, Maryland, where the original 300 boys had been weeded down to less than 100.

Over the next three days Wills pitched to fifteen batters and once again struck out everyone he faced. He also won every sprint race he was in. He was on cloud nine when a scout for the New York Giants asked to see him.

"Wills," the scout said, "I like you and I'd like to sign you, but I just can't do it. The front office would never go for it. If you were two inches taller and twenty pounds heavier, I wouldn't hesitate."

So that's how it was going to be. Everywhere he went they were going to say he was too small. Hadn't he proved that size doesn't matter? Hadn't he shown them in football and baseball that he was better than all the guys who were bigger? Didn't his high school football coach say, over and over, "It's not the size of the dog in the fight, it's the size of the fight in the dog?"

Discouraged, Maury walked out of the camp with no professional contract and no hope of ever getting one. He had just about decided to give up the idea of playing professional baseball when a Dodger representative came to his house and offered him a contract and a modest bonus of $500, which made Wills worth a little more than $3 a pound. Maury jumped at the offer. He had married his high school sweetheart, Gertrude Elliot, when they were seniors, and they were expecting a child. The money would come in handy.

In the spring of 1951 Maury Wills headed for the Dodger's camp at Vero Beach with pride and happiness. He was a professional baseball player and, although he was assigned to the minor league section, he was in a big league camp. Occasionally he would get a glimpse of Jackie Robinson, Duke Snider, Pee Wee Reese, Roy Campanella, Don Newcombe and other Dodger stars and it gave him a feeling of importance.

On that first day in camp the minor leaguers were assembled and told to go to the position they played. Wills started for the pitcher's mound, until he noticed a huge crowd gathering there. He glanced out and saw only one player at shortstop. He headed for shortstop.

Impressed with his speed, the Dodgers assigned Wills to Hornell in the Pony League as an infielder in 1951. After four years, he had moved up slowly in the Dodger organization. Each year he got a small increase in salary, and with what he picked up playing winter ball, he was

able to provide for his growing family, which now num-
bered three children. But he was still a long way from
making big money.

Maury had stolen 164 bases and never batted lower
than .279 in four minor league seasons, but he was not
advancing as rapidly as he expected. He was being swal-
lowed up in the river of talent that flowed freely through
the Dodger farm system.

In 1955, after a good year at Pueblo, he was pro-
moted to Fort Worth in the Texas League. There Wills ran
into his first serious setback. His average slipped to .202
and he stole only twelve bases. It was unanimously agreed
by the Dodger farm department that Maury had found his
level of competition. If he could not hit Texas League
pitching, how could he ever hit major league pitching? The
original reports on him were being corroborated. But the
Dodgers did not know that Maury had undergone a season
of mental strain. He had been the first Negro ever to play
for Fort Worth. And in 1955, nine years after Jackie
Robinson broke into organized baseball, Maury Wills was
subjected to the same pressures and the same harassments
Robinson suffered in his first years.

The following year he was sent down a notch, back to
Pueblo, and he responded with an outstanding year, earning a promotion to Seattle in the Pacific Coast League.
Except for Fort Worth, he never had a bad year in the
minor leagues, but it seemed nobody up there in the Dodger
front office even knew he existed. Each spring he went to
Vero Beach with confidence and the hope that someone
would spot him, but they never did. Reese was close to
retiring and the Dodgers were searching for his successor,

but there were always five or six shortstops mentioned before Wills' name.

In 1958 Maury was sent to Spokane. He fell in love with the area and moved his wife and five children there, settling down to what appeared to be a long career as a minor league shortstop. In mid-season Maury got his first break in eight years. It came in the form of a burly, swarthy-faced, fiery leader who was born in Birmingham, Alabama, and lived in Fort Worth.

His name was Bobby Bragan and he was named manager of Spokane in July. Bragan, who had spent a short and undistinguished career in the major leagues, was one of the brightest, most imaginative, most inventive young baseball minds around.

One night, a short time after he arrived at Spokane, Bragan watched his team take batting practice. He saw Wills take his usual right-handed swings, then jump around and take a couple of cuts left-handed. His stroke, Bragan noticed, was smooth and true.

"Maury," Bragan said, "have you ever tried batting left-handed before?"

"No, Bobby," Wills said, "I never gave it a thought."

"You might have hit on something. The way you can get down the line to first base, it could mean twenty more hits a year for you. That could be your ticket to the big leagues. Do you think you can do it?"

"I'd like to give it a try."

"All right. Come out a little earlier tomorrow and we'll work on it."

For three days Bragan worked with Wills, and on the fourth day Bobby said: "Now you're a switch hitter. You bat left-handed whenever a right-hander is pitching."

It was not exactly that easy. Batting left-handed, Maury could make contact consistently, but he still felt awkward at bat and had little power. He adopted a style of slapping down at the ball and taking off for first as fast as his legs could carry him. He didn't become an immediate sensation, but he could feel himself improving daily. Batting from the left side, he began to beat out ground balls to the infield that used to be routine outs when he hit right-handed.

After a slow start, Wills pushed his batting average up. He finished the season with a .253 mark, then packed his bags and headed for winter ball in Venezuela to continue the experiment.

For anyone not accustomed to it, the weather in Venezuela is unbearably hot. So hot, in fact, that they scheduled only three or four games a week. On the other days the players just loafed around the air-conditioned hotels. Not Maury Wills. He spent every day at the ballpark hitting left-handed. If he could not get a teammate to throw to him, he brought in a few kids who hung around the ballpark. But he hit, hit, hit until his hands hurt. He did not miss a day batting left-handed that entire winter.

Now he could feel it coming—the coordination, the strength, the comfort and, mostly, the confidence. He was convinced he could do the job batting left-handed. That was why he was so stunned and hurt that day in 1959 when Jim Campbell said: "I'm sorry, Maury. We're sending you back to the Dodgers."

Soon the hurt and disappointment gave way to resignation. At least he had been given a chance and he was grateful for that chance, for having been in a big league camp, for having been treated like a big leaguer.

Going back to the Dodgers would not be so bad at that. He knew he would play that season in Spokane, and Spokane was home to Wills. His family was there and it meant he could spend half the season with his wife and children. Returning to Spokane also meant going back to Bobby Bragan, the first manager to take an interest in him, to work with him. Now he could repay Bobby for all his work because he knew he had become a better hitter.

In a way, he even convinced himself that he was happy being in the minor leagues. Kind of like being the highest of those who flunked. He wasn't making big money, but he was making a decent living and with a wife and five children, he could not afford to be choosy.

"After eight years," Maury says, "you kind of lose that burning desire. You mellow, you become conditioned. I had so many ups and downs in my minor league career, one more didn't bother me. I had become resigned that I would never play shortstop for the Dodgers, but if I couldn't do that, I could become the best shortstop in the Pacific Coast League.

"I was close to quitting a hundred times, but each time I talked myself out of it. Where else could I make as much money as I was making and do something I loved as much as baseball? I knew I wouldn't quit. I couldn't quit. There was only one thing for me to do—go back to Spokane and play as long as they wanted me, and make myself into the best shortstop in the minor leagues."

Wills was happy to be back with Bragan, and his joy was reflected in his play. He knew he was improving at bat and now, finally, he could see evidence of that improvement. The season was a third old and Maury was tearing up the league with a .313 average and 25 stolen bases.

Meanwhile, the Dodgers were having their problems at shortstop. Neither Don Zimmer nor Bobby Lillis were doing the job. Rumors grew stronger that Wills would be called up to the big club. Wills asked Bragan about the rumors.

"I didn't want to tell you because I didn't want to get your hopes up," Bragan said, "but I recommended you to Buzzie Bavasi just the other day. It won't be long now. I think you'll be hearing from him soon."

He heard on June 1. Bavasi called and instructed Wills to join the Dodgers in Milwaukee. After eight and a half years of trying, he had made it to the big leagues.

Making it *to* the big leagues is not quite the same as making it *in* the big leagues. Once he came up, Maury did nothing to indicate he was there to stay. He failed to hit in his first twelve times at bat, and through the months of June and July he alternated at shortstop with Zimmer. Finally, in the middle of August, Wills became the regular shortstop, not so much because he earned it, but because Zimmer failed. Don was also not hitting, and Wills at least was a much better fielder.

The Dodgers entered a crucial three-game series against the Giants. Maury slammed seven hits in thirteen times at bat, scored four runs and was named the most valuable player of the series. That was the start. He finished out the year as the regular shortstop, batted a respectable .260 and helped the Dodgers get into the World Series. And he turned in the outstanding defensive play of the Series to help the Dodgers beat the Chicago White Sox.

The following winter dragged for Maury Wills. He could hardly wait to get to Vero Beach. He was a regular now and he expected to be treated accordingly. Instead, when he arrived, he was again assigned to the minor league annex. Apparently he had not won the job. Nothing he had done in the last six weeks in 1959 seemed to mean a thing.

Maury read in the newspapers that manager Walter Alston was concerned with his shortstop problem. Rumors spread that the Dodgers were trying to trade for an established shortstop, which did very little for Maury's peace of mind. He continued to work hard that spring to prove he deserved the job, but Alston was not convinced. Maury still had to beat out Don Zimmer, Bob Lillis and Charlie Smith.

A week before the season opened, Zimmer was traded to the Cubs. Smith had eliminated himself as a shortstop candidate and Alston, unable to swing a trade for a shortstop, announced he would alternate Wills and Lillis at the position. It was not the way Maury planned it, but now there was only one man to beat.

Maury soon won the job on the strength of his fielding, but it was a hollow victory. He was having more trouble than ever with his bat. Alston began taking him out for a pinch hitter in the seventh and eighth innings; then in the fifth and sixth innings. Discouraged and disappointed, Maury looked for a sympathetic ear for his problems and discovered coach Pete Reiser.

"He takes me out earlier and earlier," Wills said. "Before long he won't start me at all."

If Maury was looking for sympathy, he would not get it from Reiser. If he was looking for help, he came to the right place. If Bragan was the key that helped get Wills to the major leagues, Reiser was the lock that kept him

there. And to understand just what Pete Reiser could im-
part to Wills, it is necessary to understand Pete Reiser.

Harold Patrick (Pete) Reiser came to the Brooklyn
Dodgers in 1941, a 22-year-old rookie with enormous potential. He was strong and fast. He could do it all—hit,
field, run and throw—and he was the Dodgers' answer to the
center fielder across the river, Joe DiMaggio.

As a rookie, Pete hit .343 and won the National
League batting title. Baseball people everywhere were
heralding him as baseball's next great hitter. With his
speed, some even speculated he was a potential .400 hitter.
But the following year Reiser smashed his head into the
center field wall while chasing a fly ball. He was out of the
lineup with a concussion for thirty games, but still managed
to hit .310. World War II interrupted his career for three
years, and when he returned in 1946 he had another run-in
with the outfield wall. Pete Reiser was never the same after
that. Anytime his name was mentioned, people shook their
heads sadly and speculated on what he might have done if
he had been able to avoid injury. He became a symbol of
courage and regret.

"Come out two hours earlier tomorrow and we'll see
what we can do," Reiser told Wills. Maury was moved by
the offer. Here was a man willing to sacrifice two hours a
day with his family just to help a young ballplayer. The
least Maury could do was work hard and try to make it
worthwhile.

Each day they would meet at the park. For an hour
and a half Reiser would throw and Wills would hit, and
for half an hour they would talk. If the hitting was neces-

sary, the talking was absolutely vital. The one thing Wills needed was to have his confidence restored. It became a familiar sight, the two of them alone in the Los Angeles Coliseum, a spacious, 100,000-seat oval, walking in the outfield, Reiser talking and Wills listening.

"Don't just think you're better than the other guy," Reiser preached. "You have to believe it."

A week passed. A week of those special sessions with Reiser. Still there was no improvement in Wills' batting; he was still being taken out early in the game. Once he argued with the home plate umpire over a called strike. It was the third inning.

"One more word out of you," the umpire said, "and you're out of the game."

"That's okay," Wills said, bitterly. "I usually leave about this time anyway."

His batting average barely above .200, Wills felt as disappointed for Reiser as he did for himself. All the time Pete was putting in, all the hours he could have spent with his family, and still no results.

"It's no use, Pete," Maury said one night. "I'm afraid I'm just wasting your time."

"You can't quit now, Maury," Reiser insisted. "You have to keep at it. These things don't come overnight. All right, so there is no improvement, but you've got to keep working. You can't get discouraged. We'll keep working and, you'll see, it will come."

And it did come. All of a sudden it came. On the thirteenth day of their special practice sessions, Wills got three straight hits. As he walked up to home plate to bat for the fourth time, he kept expecting to hear Alston's voice come from behind him, calling him back for a pinch hitter. But he did not hear Alston's voice, and he stepped up to the plate and lined his fourth straight hit. The next day he got two more hits, the day after three more and a few days later he got four hits. It had come to him like the touch of a magic wand. Instead, he had been touched by Pete Reiser's magic words and by his own hard work and years of practice. And he did not stop working when he started hitting. Eventually Alston moved Wills up to the lead-off position in the batting order and, little by little, he gave Maury more freedom on the bases. Sometimes he even let him run on his own.

It was Reiser who helped Wills become a great base stealer, too. Pete had been an exceptional base stealer in his early days and he passed on vital tips on how to run bases. His most important tip was a philosophy of stealing. "When you get on first," Reiser kept repeating during those half-hour talk sessions which had become routine by now, "know you're going to second. Know you can beat the pitcher and the catcher and the two of them combined. You have to have an inner conceit to be a successful base stealer. You have to know you are better than either the pitcher or the catcher."

Maury batted .295 in 1960 and led the league in stolen bases with fifty. He was on his way. He was a regular when he went to Vero Beach in the spring of 1961 and, for the first time, was assigned to the major league annex. No other stortstop was mentioned in camp that spring. Wills had beaten off all the competition and the job was his to keep. He followed up with another good year—.282 and a league-leading 35 steals—but he was far from satisfied. He knew he could do better.

That winter he read a book by Ty Cobb, the greatest base stealer of them all. Cobb held the record of 96 steals in a season, a record most baseball men felt certain would never be approached.

"I read that book seven times," Maury says, "looking for tips on how to steal bases. Whenever I read it, I felt like Cobb was talking to me on every page. It was as if he was saying: 'Now Maury, you've got to put pressure on that pitcher. You've got to make him conscious of you out there.'"

Walter Alston turned Wills loose in 1962. In an unusual display of confidence in a base runner, the manager gave Maury permission to steal anytime he felt he could make it. With that privilege, Wills went on a base stealing rampage. He stole just about every time he got on base. By mid-season he had 45 steals and people were beginning to compare him with Cobb. It was practically impossible to throw him out. He was stealing ten bases for every eleven attempts. The opposition could do nothing to stop him, although they tried.

He stole on pitchouts. He stole when everyone in the park knew he would be running. Pitchers constantly violated the balk rule which requires a full second stop after the stretch. In San Francisco they watered the base paths until they were a quagmire, hoping to slow Wills down. Nothing worked.

On September 7 he stole four bases against the Pirates.

He now had 82 steals, breaking the National League record of 80 set in 1911 by Bob Bescher of the Cincinnati Reds. He ran so much that his legs were bruised from his ankles to his hips from sliding and from being hit by errant throws. The pain in his legs was so severe that he felt he could not go on any longer. Again he went to Reiser for sympathy. Again he got none.

"I think I'll take it easy, Pete, until the pain lets up."

"Get a good jump for a change," Reiser said. "Then you can steal standing up. You won't have to slide."

It was Reiser's way of saying he could not let up, he would have to go harder, not easier. He would have to concentrate so completely on stealing that he would not notice the pain.

"You can sit around and think how much you're hurting or you can forget about the pain and think about the ball game," Reiser said. "Which do you want to do?"

There really wasn't any choice.

Now it appeared Maury had an excellent chance to break Cobb's record, but there was one catch. Cobb had stolen his 96 bases in 156 games. The National League had expanded in 1962 and they had a 162-game schedule, giving Maury six more games to break the record. Just the year before, the Yankees' Roger Maris had used 162 games to hit 61 home runs; baseball commissioner Ford C. Frick ruled an asterisk would be placed alongside Maris' 61 home runs in the record books, indicating he broke Babe Ruth's historic record of 60 with the aid of eight extra games. Wills wanted no part of an asterisk. He wanted to break Cobb's record within 156 games.

Game number 156 came in St. Louis on September 23.
Maury had 95 steals. He needed one to tie and two to break
Cobb's record of 96 within the non-asterisk limit of games.
It was not going to be easy.

The pitcher for the Cardinals was Larry Jackson.
Maury had never been very successful hitting against Jackson, and you had to get on first base before you could steal
second. Also, the Dodgers were involved in a tight battle
with the San Francisco Giants for the National League pennant, and Maury knew he would have to subordinate his
personal goals for the good of the team. But just before the
game Alston gave him the inspiration he needed.

"If you get on, little man, take second," Alston said.

Fortified with that bit of encouragement, Wills went
out after his record. In the first inning he failed to get on
base. In the third he singled and, although the Dodgers
trailed by a run, he lit out for second on the first pitch and
made it easily. He had 96. One to go. He failed to hit in
the fifth inning, but in the seventh he singled again. There
was no need to steal, really, since the Cardinals led, 11–2,
but he had the word from the manager. He knew he would
try, and everyone in the ballpark knew he would try, including the pitcher, catcher and shortstop, who would most
likely handle the throw. The question was on which pitch
would he try?

Jackson stretched . . . looked over at first . . . and
pitched. Wills did not go. He had made up his mind to try
something different. He danced far off first base and waited
until the pitch was in the catcher's glove . . . then he took
off. He hoped the catcher and shortstop would relax when

he did not break with the pitch, and he was right. He capitalized on the momentary lapse to steal second base easily. It was his 97th steal. The record was his.

Wills finished the season with 104 steals in 117 attempts. He batted .299 and played in each of the Dodgers' 165 games (including three play-off games). The Dodgers lost the pennant in a play-off to the Giants, but it was Wills who took them as far as they went. For his contribution, the man once considered too small by the Giants was named the 1962 National League Most Valuable Player over Willie Mays, over Don Drysdale, over Frank Robinson, over everybody.

Maury Wills became a star of the highest magnitude, but it was not easy. Sometimes people forget, but Maury Wills will never forget the years of work and struggle and frustration that went into his success.

He is the example of what hard work and determination can do. It has become the vogue in recent years for speedy little infielders who cannot hit to turn around and try switch-hitting, and all because of Maury Wills, the patron saint of the little man.

Maury Wills is not the player you notice first. He is the smallest man on the field. He is not the fastest and he is far from the strongest, but when he plays, it is Maury Wills you remember after all the others have been forgotten. He plays with a fierce intensity because there is an enormous pride in this little man that sometimes seems too big to be housed in a body which stands five feet, ten inches tall and weighs scarcely more than 160 pounds. He is belligerent and defiant and vain. But it is this belligerence, defiance and vanity that makes him excel where others fail, and makes him carry on when others quit. It is this hunger to be the best that makes him the best.

That is Maury Wills, and that is why he never gave up even though he knew every major league team had a file card on him that said, "Too small for major league baseball."

"My contention," he has said, "is that you don't have to be blessed with size to compete on an equal basis with larger boys. It's what you have inside that really counts."

Size is not important. Desire is, and so is patience. For Maury, it was necessary to be patient, to work hard, to struggle for eight and a half years in the minor leagues until others were convinced, as he is, that size is not important.

"I have no regrets about the eight years I spent in the minor leagues," he says. "Rather than be bitter about those eight years and say they were wasted, I like to look at them as years spent getting a good foundation in baseball. I don't feel that I was mistreated. Those eight years gave me the maturity to cope with what I had to cope with, and they gave me the extra knowledge of the game that is so essential. Look at it another way. If I had been called up four or five years earlier, I wouldn't have been ready for it. I know I wouldn't have made it and I would have gone up and down and eventually been released. Staying down, playing regularly in the minor leagues, I learned. And when the time came for me to go to the major leagues, I was ready."

There is also the Maury Wills code or the Maury Wills

philosophy that is applicable not only to baseball, but to everything in life.

"You can accomplish almost anything if you are willing to work hard enough. The proper mental attitude can be acquired. If you're motivated enough, you can learn to do anything, and when the going gets rough you prove what you have inside. I've been very lucky. Lucky to be with the Dodgers, lucky to have had teammates who helped me. That's the truth, but it's not the entire truth. I've gotten opportunities, what you might call lucky breaks, but I've been prepared to take advantage of my opportunities."

Branch Rickey said, "Luck is the residue of design." Maury Wills puts it another way. "Luck," he says, "is opportunity meeting preparation."

PETE GOGOLAK

"This is a great country. Here you have every opportunity to make something of yourself."

The morning of December 1, 1956, came up damp and raw in the troubled city of Budapest, Hungary. Outside it was still dark. Inside a two-story building, in a room on the top floor, two young boys were sleeping in a large bed, a mound of blankets piled on top of them against the chill that penetrated the poorly heated brick house. A man slipped quietly into the room, groping his way in the darkness. Gently he shook the older boy until his eyes were open and the boy looked at the man sleepily.

"Get dressed, quickly," the man said.

"What is it, papa?"

"We must go away now," the man replied.

"Is something wrong?"

"No, my son," the father said, "nothing is wrong. But we are leaving. We are going far away."

The words "far away" cut through the boy's sleepiness and suddenly he was wide awake. He had known this day would eventually come, and he looked forward to it with excitement mixed with apprehension and sadness. He often dreamed of one day going to live in a far-off land such as England or America. But now, climbing out from under the warm covers, the winter cold chilling his frail, young body, there was a feeling of sadness as he thought of leaving all his friends and never seeing them again.

The boy did not know where he was going or why his father had decided to leave so hastily, but he knew better than to ask questions. He had faith that whatever his father decided must be the right thing.

The father, John Gogolak, had been a successful and prominent physician, for years one of Budapest's leading citizens. While he never attained great wealth, he provided well for his wife Sarolta and their two boys, Peter, age 14, and Charles, 12. A symbol of Dr. Gogolak's stature and financial security was the two-story brick building he owned and in which his family lived comfortably and happily. The accommodations were better than those of most people of Budapest, and while some of Peter's friends had only one pair of shoes and often went without food, Peter and his brother always had enough to eat and enjoyed the luxury of three pairs of shoes each.

Then came 1945. The Great War had ended in Europe and the Communists took control of the Hungarian government. Everything was changed. The Communists said there was a housing shortage, so they confiscated Dr. Gogolak's two-story brick house and issued the proclamation that all property now belonged to the new People's Republic. Another family was moved into the first floor of the house; the Gogolaks were permitted to live on the second floor, for which they paid rent to the government.

Peter was three and his brother was just an infant when the Communists came to Budapest. They grew up in fear and enslavement. They had become accustomed to seeing soldiers and tanks parade through the streets of town. They witnessed friends and neighbors savagely beaten and dragged off by soldiers, never to be heard from again.

On October 23, 1956, Hungarian freedom fighters staged a gallant revolt in an attempt to regain control of the government from the Communists. But, eleven days later, with the help of Russian troops, the revolt was crushed and the people of Hungary plunged once again into fear and despair. The failure of the uprising convinced John Gogolak that the time had come to take his family out of the troubled land. There was an opportunity to escape because the country was still in chaos and turmoil after the brief, violent, destructive revolt. Dr. Gogolak did not want to leave the land of his birth. He loved Hungary, but the Hungary of 1956 was not the Hungary he had known as boy and man.

It takes a special brand of courage for a man in his forties to abandon his professional practice, his home, his friends, his customs, his country and what was left of his worldly possessions in order to search for a new home, a new life in a land thousands of miles from the only world he had ever known. Dr. John Gogolak found that courage on a cold December morning. He found it because he wanted to provide a better future for his two young sons and for the third child who would be born in just a few months. When that child was born, Dr. Gogolak wanted him to come into a world that was free, a world where you did not go to sleep each night afraid that you would be awakened by a knock on the door and carried away.

For many months he had been making plans for his escape. With the help of friends he arranged to cross the border into Austria, from where he would eventually head for Australia. A friend told him Australia was the easiest place for a European doctor to obtain a license to practice his profession.

When all the arrangements were made he waited until the time was right. Then, on this cold December morning, he awakened his family to tell them the time had come. As a dutiful son, young Peter did exactly what his father instructed. He dressed quickly and quietly, making certain to wear his warmest suit and his best pair of shoes. The family would not take any extra clothing—baggage would arouse suspicion and endanger their chances of making a successful escape.

Breakfast was waiting for Peter after he had dressed. He ate hurriedly and silently, and when he was finished his father said to the family: "Do not talk. Just follow me." A taxi was waiting for them in front of the house. The driver pulled away without speaking a word, and Peter turned and looked at his house for the last time. The taxi moved slowly through the streets, and Peter could see dozens of the 5,000 Russian tanks that had come during the revolution.

Soon the cab pulled up at the railroad station. Peter's father paid the driver and led the way onto the train. The family found seats together and waited in silence until the wheels of the train began to roll and they slowly moved out of the station. They hardly spoke at all, and when they did it was softly and casually. Peter sat quietly, staring out the window, watching the trees and farm houses as the train rumbled by. He thought of the friends he would never see again and he felt sad. He also thought of the soldiers and the tanks, a painful reminder of the life he was leaving. About that he had no regrets.

Peter turned from the window and looked at his father. Seeing him sitting there looking carefree and calm gave Peter a feeling of contentment and confidence. He turned back to the window, filled with anticipation. He imagined himself in his new home, in his new country, playing with new friends, going to a new school, learning a new language.

They had been traveling for several hours when the train came to a stop. His father motioned to his family to follow him. A man was waiting at the station and they went with him to a farmhouse, where they were greeted with warm, tender embraces. Although Peter had never seen these people before, he felt at ease in their presence. They seemed to be friends of his father, who had very many friends. Peter, his mother and brother were invited to sit down to dinner. While they ate his father stood off in a corner, talking to a strange man whom Peter had not noticed when he first entered the house.

Dinner was over and it had become dark outside. Dr. Gogolak, who had only nibbled at his food, said to them: "Come, it's time to go. We have a long journey ahead."

They put on their coats and his father's friends embraced each of them again. The woman of the house, who had prepared the dinner, grabbed Peter and there were tears in her eyes as she hugged and kissed him. His father thanked his friends for their hospitality, and they stepped out into the night.

It was damp outside and the ground was muddy from the rain that had fallen earlier in the day. Peter noticed they were no longer alone. They had been joined by the man his father had talked with during dinner. The stranger was a guide who was paid to help them on their journey. Peter knew this was dangerous because many guides, pretending to be friendly to people trying to escape Hungary, had turned out to be government informers. It was a risk Peter knew had to be taken. The stranger was familiar with the area and Peter's father was not.

They walked slowly and quietly out of the city and into the hay fields. They passed several Army barracks, but the few soldiers they saw ignored them. It was as if they were a family just out for an evening stroll.

In the distance Peter heard the rumble of tanks and, occasionally, his heart beat faster at the sound of rifle fire. But Peter and his family continued to walk with purpose and with confidence. He had no doubt they would reach their destination without being captured.

They had been walking for hours through the muddy hay fields, their bodies tired and aching with pain, their shoes covered with mud, when they came to a barren field that stretched for one hundred yards. Peter knew exactly where they were. He had heard his father speak many times about this field. It was called "no man's land" because of its emptiness, and he knew at the end of that field was the Austrian border—the gateway to freedom.

Before the revolution it was almost impossible to cross the border, made inviolate by an electric fence, land mines and guards. But during the revolution most of the mines had been detonated, the fence was torn down and there were no longer enough soldiers available to patrol the border. Hungarian refugees by the hundreds fled from the land to find safety and political asylum in the free countries of the world. Still, Peter was aware that the most difficult part of the journey was before them.

Flares exploded at ten-minute intervals, lighting the land as if it were midday. Each time a flare popped, the five of them stopped and huddled closely together to give the appearance they were bales of hay. When the light faded the tiring journey resumed.

They successfully crossed "no man's land" into Austria, but Peter knew they were not yet safe. It would be hours before they could rest. They continued walking, their pace slackening as fatigue slowly overtook their bodies. In the distance Peter could see bright lights, and he knew it was Vienna twinkling a welcome as a haven for its oppressed neighbors.

Several times, his mother stopped, breathing deeply as if to muster the courage and strength to continue. She was tired and in pain, and once she stumbled and almost fell. His father said to him, "Peter, grab your mother's arm." Peter clutched one arm, his father the other, and together they half carried, half dragged her. It made Peter feel strong and courageous and grown up.

The lights of Vienna continued to shine brightly in the distance like some remote castle that would never be reached. They kept walking, but the lights seemed never to get any closer. They crossed a railroad track . . . then another . . . and another. Finally they realized they were crossing the same railroad track. They had been walking in a circle. A feeling of frustration overcame them when they thought of the time that had been lost, the precious energy that had been spent in vain.

Finally they came to a small road, and beyond it they could see a group of people huddled around a truck. Peter's heart skipped rapidly in fear, but as they grew closer he could see a huge white square on the side of the truck, and in the middle of the square was a red cross. They had reached the end of their journey! Peter turned to glance at his mother. Tears of joy were streaming down her face.

They had left everything behind to start a new life. They did not know what lay before them, where and when their journey would end, but they knew one thing . . . one very important thing. They knew the reason for the danger they had willingly faced, the pain and fatigue they had endured. At last, they were free.

The Red Cross cared for Peter's mother. They put her in a hospital to help rebuild her strength. A week passed and his father said it was time to move on. They went to Munich, Germany, where Peter's father had some friends who had arranged airplane passage for the family. One of these friends convinced Dr. Gogolak to change his original plans, and when his father told Peter of the change, the boy could not control his excitement. They were not going to Australia. They were going to the United States.

The flight was unbearably long for Peter and his family, but finally the huge airplane dipped its wings as it prepared to descend. Slowly it reduced altitude, and Peter stared out the window almost in disbelief. He could see the Statue of Liberty, that proud lady of freedom majestically holding a torch of liberty in her right hand. Then he saw a wondrous sight . . . buildings taller than he had ever seen in his life, hundreds of them stretching out as far as his eye could see.

On January 5, 1957, one month and four days after they had set out from Budapest, they landed in Camp Kilmer, New Jersey, an old Army camp which served as a reception center and temporary home for refugees. Peter's father left them to go in search of work and a home. After several weeks he returned with news. He had found a job in a hospital in Ogdensburg, a pleasant town of 16,000 people near the St. Lawrence River in upstate New York. He would go to Ogdensburg to begin work and look for a place to live, and after he had made the necessary arrangements he would send for the family.

Spring of 1957 and Pete Gogolak arrived at Ogdensburg simultaneously. With spring came a rebirth of nature. The last of the winter's snow had melted, buds were beginning to appear on bushes and the foliage was turning a cool, lush green. It was a time of rebirth for Pete Gogolak, too.

It was not easy at first adjusting to a new life. Peter spoke no English and nobody in Ogdensburg spoke Hungarian. Since they were not about to learn, Peter knew he would have to learn English. His father sent him off to Ogdensburg Free Academy with these words of advice: "Work hard and study hard, my son. This is a great country. Here you have every opportunity to make something of yourself. But you can only do it with hard work."

Peter heeded the advice. Each night he sat down with a dictionary and his father helped him learn the strange new language. He set for himself the difficult goal of learning 25 words every night. Within months he could converse adequately, though haltingly, in English. Because of the language barrier he was put back in the same grade when he enrolled in school for the fall semester. But, with hard work and determination, he managed to make up three years' work in the next two years.

His father proudly watched the boy grow to manhood during those two years. Never had he seen Peter so happy, and if he had doubts about leaving his homeland, watching his boys grow up erased them from his mind.

Peter grew tall and strong, and by the time he entered his junior year in high school, in the fall of 1958, he had become completely adapted to his new life. He was a handsome boy with a strong, sharp chin, bright eyes and blonde hair. Except for a slight accent, he was as American as Jack Armstrong. He looked like an American, dressed like an American, thought like an American. His friendliness, his outgoing personality and his willingness to mix with others made him one of the most popular boys in school. Only one thing disturbed him. There was a void in his life. He had always been athletic and in Hungary had been one of the best soccer players on a team that won the junior European championship. Unfortunately Ogdensburg Free Academy had no soccer team, and Peter was reluctant to try the American sports which he did not fully understand.

He was aware that the most popular boys in school, the boys who received the greatest attention, played on the foot-

ball team. Someone suggested he try out for the team. He
knew the rules required body contact, but he was bigger
than most of the boys he admired, and stronger too, and he
certainly had no fear of injury. He went out for the team,
although he knew so little about the game he did not even
know it involved kicking.

Because of his size—he was 6 feet 2 and 200 pounds—
the coach made him an end. He worked hard to learn the
new game, and while he never imagined he would get anything out of football except competition, camaraderie with
his teammates and a feeling of belonging, it made him
proud to be a part of the team.

On the day before the first game of the season, the
coach asked for players to try out as kickers. Pete joined the
group and waited while five other boys kicked. He noticed
the American boys had a very unusual way of kicking. They
faced the ball head-on, raced up and met it with their toes.
Peter imagined it must be very painful. In soccer you
kicked the ball with your instep.

Now it was Peter's turn to kick. He stood off to the side
at a 45-degree angle to the ball.

"Hey, Pete," he heard a voice shout, "you're not going
to kick that way, are you?"

Before the words were out, Peter had made contact and
the ball sailed far down the field. He kicked several more,
each one as far as the first and much farther than anyone
else was able to kick it. But he could not get any height on
the ball. The coach selected Peter to do the kicking off, but
for extra points and field goals he picked another boy. It
disturbed Peter because he knew he could kick better than
the other boy.

Each night Peter stayed to practice his kicking. The
other players would watch him, laughing when he lined up

in that awkward position and kicked the ball with the inside of his foot. Sometimes he became so embarrassed by the laughter and the comments that he went to a deserted cow pasture to practice his kicking. He practiced every day the following summer. When he could, he took a teammate or his brother Charlie or a little neighborhood boy with him to shag the ball, but usually he would have to kick and chase all by himself. Pete soon learned that the life of a kicker is a lonely one, but he knew what it was like to be lonely and, sometimes, he welcomed the chance to be alone with his thoughts of the future.

By the time he was a senior the hours of practice had paid off. He now could kick high as well as far and, when he proved his ability, he was allowed to try extra points, then field goals. Before long colleges all around the country were getting fantastic reports of a high school boy in upstate New York who was compiling an amazing record by kicking a football soccer style.

One day Pete arrived home from practice to find a letter waiting for him. It was from the director of admissions at Cornell University. He anxiously tore open the envelope and scanned the letter. A few words jumped out at him. "Accepted . . . Cornell University . . . fall semester . . . 1960."

Although his reputation as a kicker preceded Pete Gogolak to Cornell, there was still some laughter the first time he attempted to kick during freshman football practice. During the season he kicked a 48-yard field goal; varsity coach Tom Harp told Pete that his days as an end were over. From then on he would be a kicker, and only a kicker. He was considered too valuable to risk injury in something so unimportant as blocking and tackling.

In three varsity seasons at Cornell, Pete made good on

54 out of 55 extra point attempts, including a collegiate record of 44 in a row. The record lasted for two years until it was broken by a Princeton place kicker who had copied the unorthodox, but newly accepted Pete Gogolak style of placekicking. The new record was 50 consecutive points after touchdown and the new soccer-style, record-breaking booter was a boy who had come to this country from Hungary. His name was Charlie Gogolak.

A place kicker who can kick extra points with consistency and, more importantly, can kick field goals from forty yards out is worth his weight in shoulder pads. He is on the high priority list of any professional football team. He is not a luxury but an absolute necessity. A good kicker can mean the difference between an also-ran and a championship team. The history of professional football is crammed with stories of championships won by a field goal or an extra point. Considering all this, it is difficult to understand why Pete Gogolak in his senior year evoked very little interest from the pros. The only explanation is a unanimous skepticism of his unusual method of kicking.

One day Harvey Johnson, director of player personnel for the Buffalo Bills of the American Football League and a former professional place kicker, decided to take a ride to Cornell to see the wonder kicker with his own eyes. When he arrived, Johnson found the playing field vacant except for Gogolak, who was practicing his kicking although the Cornell season had ended. Johnson introduced himself and asked Gogolak if he would give a demonstration of his kicking ability. Pete consented, and Harvey Johnson stepped aside to watch.

"Excuse me, Mr. Johnson," Pete said, "you're standing in my way."

Embarrassed, but more curious and skeptical than

ever, Johnson moved. Gogolak kicked a few short ones for a starter, then backed up. When Pete started to tee the ball up at the 50-yard line, Johnson said, "That's enough."

"I figured," Johnson said later, "he was going to cost us enough already. Anyway, I was convinced."

Buffalo signed Gogolak, and if there were any skeptics left in the world, Pete won them over in his first exhibition game as a Bills' rookie. He kicked a 57-yard field goal, at the time the longest ever kicked by a professional.

In his rookie year Gogolak missed only one extra point in 46 attempts, and he kicked 19 field goals in 28 tries. But he was disappointed and disillusioned when it came time to negotiate for his 1965 contract. He felt his talents were not fully appreciated, although he was the league's second leading scorer with 102 points. He decided to play out his option. That meant playing the entire season without a contract so that he might become a free agent in 1966 and negotiate with another team for a better contract. It was a big gamble, especially for one with so little professional experience, but Pete displayed the kind of courage he had shown so often before in his young life. He made good on all 31 of his extra point attempts and kicked 28 field goals in 46 tries. Again, he was the second leading scorer in the league, this time with 115 points, and he was free to sign with another team.

Pete felt justified in his self-appraisal. Even though he spends a total of about six minutes a season on the playing field, he practices his kicking six hours daily. His contribution to the success of the Bills could not be measured in playing time or be evaluated in dollars and cents.

In 1966 he signed with the New York Giants of the National Football League, who could hardly fail to appre-

ciate Pete's talents. While Gogolak was making good on
.655 of his field goals in 1965, the Giants had scored only
4 three-pointers in 24 attempts.

The rewards for the hours he spent practicing and the
years he struggled have been enormous—and not only for
the money he has made and the fame he has earned. The
greatest reward came on Sunday, November 8, 1964, in
New York's Shea Stadium. A crowd of 60,300, the largest
in the history of the American Football League, had
jammed the new stadium to see the Bills take on the New
York Jets. Among the fans were a doctor, his wife and two
of his three sons.

Early that morning John Gogolak and his family had
climbed into their car and driven four hours on the New
York State Thruway from their new home in Saratoga
Springs to Flushing, New York. They watched the New York
Jets take an early 7–0 lead. Then, late in the second period,
the Bills scored a touchdown, and Pete Gogolak kicked the
extra point that tied the game. With 9:49 gone in the third
period, they saw Pete soccer-kick one 47 yards to put his
team ahead, and twelve minutes later they watched him kick
a 33-yarder. The game ended with Buffalo ahead, 20–7.
Pete Gogolak was the hero, and Dr. John Gogolak swelled
with parental pride. He wanted to tell everyone around him,
"that's my son."

If Dr. Gogolak was proud, so was his hero son. Inside
the Buffalo clubhouse he talked with reporters.

"Just seven years ago," he said, "we flew over New
York for the first time, alone and afraid. We saw all those
tall buildings and all those people for the first time. Now,
here is my whole family in New York City, watching me
play professional football. It is all so unbelievable."

JIM HURTUBISE

"He kept saying 'I'll race again, Doc.
You'll see'."

Suddenly he was awake, and the familiar rocking motion
instinctively told Jim Hurtubise that he was riding in a car.
But this time it was different. This time instead of sitting in
the driver's seat, his hands firmly clutching the steering
wheel and the car hurtling around an oval at rapid speed, he
was lying flat on his back. He looked up. A man dressed

in a white gown was bending over him, wiping perspiration from his brow.

"He's a doctor," Jim thought, "and I'm riding in an ambulance, so I must have been hurt, but I can't remember. . . ."

There was a throbbing in his hands. Jim Hurtubise looked down at them, and what he saw made him turn his eyes away in horror. His hands were red and scarred and they looked like mittens of seared flesh and his fingers . . . his fingers . . . where were his fingers? Now it all came back to him in a flash. Now he remembered.

It was a bright, sunny Sunday, June 7, 1964, and he had come to the little Milwaukee suburb of West Allis, Wisconsin, to compete in the fifteenth annual 100-mile Rex Mays Classic at the Wisconsin State Fair Speedway. He had come full of confidence and hope, for he had been driving very well in recent months and his stature in the field of auto racing was on the rise. So was his bank balance. He was competing against all the top drivers now . . . A. J. Foyt, Jimmy Clark, Rodger Ward . . . and he was winning his share of races. It had been a long, hard climb to the top, but he had made it and now he was full of confidence. He felt certain he would pick up a big check this day, maybe even the $3,300 first-place money.

Jim Hurtubise was considered one of the best young drivers in the business and, at 32, he had many good years ahead of him. He was a young man going places. He was also one of the most well-liked drivers in the game, well-liked by other drivers and by fans. Everybody took to Jim easily because he was that kind of guy. Part of it was his pleasant personality and part his gameness and fearlessness on the race track. Hercules they called him because of his size—or lack of it. He stood 5'6" and weighed 150 pounds so they called him Hercules, or Herky for short.

The race was about to start and Herky's stomach flip-flopped with anticipation. It always did at the start of a race when he heard the familiar buzz of excitement from the crowd and the sound of drivers revving their motors. He had qualified third, which put him on the pole in the second tier behind A. J. Foyt and Rodger Ward. He threw his car into gear and began rolling, slowly accelerating. Now he was moving at a rapid pace, zooming down the first straight-away. Up ahead he could see the green flag that signalled the start of the race. And then they were off, the whirr of speeding cars accompanied by a roar of satisfaction from the crowd of 36,285 loud and anxious fans.

On the race track Jim Hurtubise is known as a charger. He slams on the gas pedal and charges to the front with exciting abandon. He puts his foot through the floorboard and tries to push to the lead early in the race and stay there.

But this time he could not get out in front, so he settled into third place. Foyt went to the top and Ward was second. Jim was content to let them set the pace. He lay a close third in his fire-red Novi, the Tombstone Life Special.

They sped around the track in the same order—Foyt in the lead, Ward second and Hurtubise third—for thirty miles. On the 31st lap Ward charged ahead to overtake Foyt for the lead, while Hurtubise maintained his position in third place. Settling into the 47th lap, Jim decided to make his move. He pushed ahead of Foyt into second place, but

A. J., reacting to the challenge, jammed down hard on his accelerator and regained second position, with Jim falling back to third once again.

They were in the 52nd lap, and as they came out of the north turn and headed into the homestretch, Herky could see another chance to move up on the leaders. Up ahead he saw Ward, in the lead car, giving ground. Jim put his foot down to the floor and made his move.

But something was wrong with Ward's car: it was slowing down perceptibly. Ahead of him Herky could see Foyt hit his brakes and swerve ever so slightly to the right in an effort to avoid hitting Ward's car . . . but Foyt could not do so. He grazed the rear of Ward's car and bounced off to the right, directly into Herky's path. There was nothing Jim could do to avoid the collision.

Jim Hurtubise ran over Foyt's right rear wheel, the front of his car punching a hole in the rear of Foyt's car. Jim bounced off and skidded crazily from the impact, smashing into the retaining wall to his right. He spun off the retaining wall and his car made a 180-degree turn. The front of Herky's car was facing oncoming traffic as he bounced off into the center of the track.

Cars sped by Jim Hurtubise, avoiding further collision, but the wheel of A. J. Foyt's car had flown off and smashed into Hurtubise's cockpit, catching Jim in the head and chest. The right front tire of Herky's car was ripped clear, and bits of his car flew into the grandstand sending spectators scattering for safety. The cap flew off his gas tank. And the impact of car-hitting-wall ruptured the fuel-line, causing the car to burst into vicious, ugly flames.

The crowd hushed in terror as the yellow light, signalling danger on the track, blinked furiously. The only sound heard was the frightening, sickening, urgent screech of an ambulance siren.

In an instant the track's emergency and safety crews and the men from Jim Hurtubise's pit crew were on the track, racing to the flaming car from three different directions, some carrying fire extinguishers. Among them was Don Hurtubise, the chief mechanic for his brother.

"Get him out, get him out," a voice shrieked in fear. "Get him out before he burns to death."

But they could not get him out. He was locked in the cockpit. The flames spit their danger and nobody could get close enough to the charred wreckage to get to Jim Hurtubise. They could only stand there, helplessly, looking at him sitting in a pool of gasoline, watching the flames engulf him, devouring his body, searing his flesh.

Finally the fire was extinguished, and three men tugged at Jim Hurtubise's scorched body to free him from the car. Instinctively, dazedly, he tried to climb back into the car, to continue the race, but they pulled him away. You could hear him moaning painfully and saying, over and over, "take it easy, take it easy, take it easy."

Then he collapsed and they pulled him away. When they put him in the ambulance, he was unconscious.

Now, riding in the ambulance with the doctor bending over him and gently wiping the perspiration from his brow, Jim was awake. When he looked at the ugly stumps that remained where once his fingers used to be, the thought that came to him was: "Oh, no. I'll never be able to drive again." He saw his career coming to an abrupt end just as it was practically beginning, just as he was hitting the big time, pocketing the big checks. He had worked so hard to get where he was and now it was over. The thought filled him with fear and frustration and a strange feeling of emptiness.

He lay there in the ambulance not saying a word. His mind raced back, remembering how it had all started for him. He was a kid again in the quiet town of North Tonawanda in upstate New York. Even then he was interested in cars. The best thing in his life was getting behind the wheel of some old jalopy, putting his foot down on the accelerator and just letting her go. It gave him a feeling of freedom.

He always had a knack for mechanical things. When he was in high school he got a job working after school in a local garage. He was a pretty good automobile mechanic. The boss told him so, and before he knew it he was not only pumping gas, he was doing repair work as well. Jim saved the money he earned at the garage, enough to buy himself an old heap. Every chance he got, he worked on his car. He souped her up and got that old thing to where she could hit 100.

On weekends Jim and a few of the fellows would go up to Buffalo to watch the stock car races and the midget races. There was never a time like that in all his life. He felt a surge of excitement sitting there watching the races, and he knew that was where he belonged, right there on the race track.

After high school Jim Hurtubise enlisted in the Coast Guard, which was very poor casting. He belonged in the Army, in a mobile unit. He was stationed in St. Petersburg, Florida, and the first chance he got he bought himself a

1934 coupe. In his spare time he began working on her. He cut her down and lightened her and started racing.

He entered a few races while in service and had enough success to consider racing for a living. When he was discharged he took up the sport in earnest. He raced in New York and Baltimore, then worked his way west, ending up in California in 1955. There he began racing open cockpit sprint cars. It was hard, frustrating work. Improvement came slowly and the money even came more slowly. But Jim Hurtubise could not be discouraged. He was doing what he loved best and he was having fun. He knew hard work would bring improvement, and improvement would bring victories and money.

From sprint cars he advanced to the International Motor Contest Association, and from there to the United States Auto Club. Then it was the fall of 1959 and Jim Hurtubise won at Sacramento. He had arrived. He was in the big leagues.

In 1960 he was invited to compete in the World Series of auto racing, the Indianapolis 500. He set a qualification record by averaging 149 miles an hour. He finished eighteenth in the race and was named Rookie of the Year. After that, Jim was one of the big boys. No track on the circuit failed to include his name among its list of invitees. And Jimmy showed them a thing or two. He won at Langhorne in 1960 and at Springfield in 1961 and 1962. He was the hottest young driver in the game. His dream, at last, was coming true.

Then it was that warm, June Sunday in Milwaukee in 1964, and his dream and his car were smashed by the north wall of the Wisconsin State Fair Speedway.

They rushed him to the West Allis Memorial Hospital but they could not treat him there. They took one look at his burns and decided he needed specialized treatment, so they contacted the Brooke Army Medical Center at Fort Sam Houston in San Antonio, Texas which has one of the finest burn centers in the world. Less than 22 hours after the accident, Jim Hurtubise was wheeled into the operating room of the San Antonio hospital. Conscious and coherent, he looked up at the doctor waiting to perform the operation.

"Hey, doc," he said, "do you think I'll be able to drive again?"

"I don't know, Jim," said Lt. Col. Walter Switzer, "you've got a pretty bad burn. But we'll do the best we can."

"He was burned on 40 percent of his body," Dr. Switzer recalled. "That's a good sized injury. The mortality rate in cases like these is about 30 percent."

The operation took seven hours. Doctors cleaned and cut away charred tissue. They took skin from Jim's chest, back and hips and grafted it to the injured areas.

"He was damaged so badly, he lost portions of his fingers," Dr. Switzer said. "The tips of his fingers were badly incinerated and his nose was completely burned off. Our biggest concern was that a dry type of gangrene would set in, in which case we would have to amputate his hands. Frankly, I was pessimistic that he would ever drive again.

"My first concern was saving his life. My second concern was saving his hands, and my third concern was putting his hands back in working order for normal things, not necessarily for driving. Our main job was to reconstruct his hands and fingers so that he would not lose the mobility of them."

But Dr. Switzer had not reckoned with old Herky's heart. The expert team at Brooke Army Medical Center saved Jim's life and they saved his hands, but where there once were fingers, there now red, raw bony claws. Still, Jim refused to be discouraged. He refused to give up hope that he would someday drive again.

"Jim is a well-motivated young man," Dr. Switzer said. "He is not the kind of individual to show emotion, and his principal anxiety was whether he would be able to drive again. Actually, that made him a better patient. He was interested in what we were doing and he cooperated with us fully. This great desire to drive again made him work very hard. I felt, subconsciously, that he would frown on the skin grafting, but he never let it show. He kept saying, 'I'll race again, doc. You'll see.' Naturally, we never tried to discourage him, although we still could find no reason to be optimistic."

After two and a half months Jim was released from the hospital, but he kept going back for skin grafts and physical therapy. He was working harder than ever. He spent hours gripping an exercise wheel to recover the movement in his fingers and hands, and he practically had to learn to walk all over again.

Sometimes the pain would be so severe it brought tears to his eyes, but old Herky would not give up. The more severe the pain, the tighter he gripped that exercise wheel, all the while pretending it was a steering wheel.

Through the pain, through the hard work, through the struggle to recapture his dream, Jim Hurtubise remained determined, philosophical and optimistic. He refused to accept the pity that was showered upon him. He refused to accept his accident as hard luck. And he refused to admit to the dangers of his profession, the thing he loved more than anything else, even life itself. Fear was alien to Jim Hurtubise's nature, and pity was for some other guy. It was not for him.

"That was really the first time I was hurt," he pointed out. "The first time I was hurt bad. It's my job, it's what I enjoy doing most. I make good money at it and I can't see any reason for quitting. You know, you can get hurt at anything. Construction workers get hurt on their job and factory workers get hurt on their job and they don't quit. They go right back to it."

Jim Hurtubise always had faith, and when he went back for his final operation and the doctors told him he would never be able to move his fingers again, he asked them to curl his fingers so they would be in position to grip a steering wheel. After he had the last of his operations, Jim Hurtubise went back to his 15-acre farm in North Tonawanda, New York, and drove a bulldozer to help put the callouses back on his hands.

He interrupted his work to return to the Wisconsin State Fair Speedway in September 1964 as a spectator. It was Jim Hurtubise Day, and thousands cheered him and pitied him. When they looked at him they shook their heads sadly. Wasn't it too bad about Jim Hurtubise? He was a great driver once, but he had driven on a race track for the last time.

Jim was warmed by the reception. He waved to the cheering crowd and vowed to himself that he would someday come back to the Wisconsin State Fair Speedway, but not as a spectator. Others doubted him, but Jim Hurtubise never had any doubt.

"I knew I would came back," he said. "I never had any doubt. The doctors told me it would take time but I'd be able to use my hands again. I believed them and I just kept working at it. They said it would take time and a lot of hard work, so I did a lot of work and got back in shape."

Week after week, with the pain sometimes so unbearable it made Jim clench and cringe in horror, he worked, wriggling the misshapen bones and flexing the muscles in his hands to regain strength and control. Improvement was slow and tedious, but Jim refused to quit.

"I figured once you're hurt that's it," he said, "You can either enjoy it or not. I knew being miserable wouldn't get me better any sooner, so I decided to enjoy it. There was nothing wrong inside my head, nothing that could change my attitude. From the minute I woke up inside the ambulance in Milwaukee, I knew I'd be back if I was physically able. It's not guts. I think it takes more guts to be a football player. There you've got body contact and those guys are out there to hit one another; they know they're going to get hit and they can get seriously hurt just by falling the wrong way. All I do is drive a car, and it's really safer than driving on a highway. At least we don't have reckless drivers on the track."

For Jim there was really little choice. He could go back to his job as a welder and spend a peaceful, comfortable, safe life with his wife and three children . . . and suffer. He would suffer because he would not be doing the thing he loved best, and he would never know if he could have made it big again on the race track.

"I intend to drive just as long as I'm able," he says. "I've just gotten to the point where I'm making big money, and my family would be well provided for if anything ever

As soon as he was released from the hospital, Jim tried his charred hands out behind the wheel of a sports car.

happened to me. My wife's a game girl. She never talked to me about quitting. She knows driving's my life."

Nine months after his accident Herky was back on the track. It was at the Trenton Fairgrounds, a mile-long paved oval in New Jersey. Incredibly, he was back behind the wheel of a racing car. He wore gloves and you could tell it hurt just to grip the wheel, but he fought back against the pain. He went out on the track to prove he could still drive, even with stumps for fingers.

"I can get the job done," he said determinedly.

He did not win at Trenton—that is, he didn't finish first—but he won a lot more than a race. He won the respect and admiration of everyone in the racing game. He challenged for the lead several times, but his car quit on him. When he finally had to pull his car out of the race, it was not because of his grip or his fingers or the pain. It was the machine that quit, not the man.

He climbed out of his car, exhaustion, pain and disappointment showing on his face, his hands hanging limply at his side. This was not the end, it was only the beginning. "They're hurting less all the time," he said bravely.

In July 1965 he was in a 200-mile stock car race. He led from the 61st mile to the 85th, gave up the lead and then regained it at the 129th mile. He kept the lead until the 199th mile. Then he was out of brakes: he had to slow down at the turns. On the last lap Norm Nelson, who owned the car Herky was driving, came barrelling through to win.

The fans condemned Nelson mercilessly. They wanted Herky to win, and they booed Nelson for what they interpreted as lack of sportsmanship in taking the race away from his partner. But Herky could not condemn Nelson. When he won he wanted it to be on his own merit, not as a result of someone else's charity. "He's out to win, too," Jim said. "There's no room for sympathy on the race track.'

Two months later he was back in Milwaukee . . . back to the Wisconsin State Fair Speedway . . . back to the scene of his horrible accident.

It was a 250-mile stock car race and it all came back to him . . . the awful memory of the crash . . . his car hurtling crazily out of control, smashing into the retaining wall . . . the fire all around him . . . the pain and the sudden fear of being trapped in an inferno with no escape . . . and the sickening feeling when he awoke in the ambulance and saw that his fingers were melted away, his hands mittens of seared flesh.

The fans would not let him forget. There were 21,350 of them there that Sunday, September 19, 1965, and they cheered at the mere mention of his name, at the very sight of him. Someone asked him if he was worried about the north wall, whether he feared he would be gun-shy when he got near it. Jim Hurtubise smiled. "I'm not worried about it at all," he said. "I just have to remember to stay away from it, that's all."

His heart beat rapidly and his stomach jumped nervously as he waited for the start of the race. When they dropped the flag Jim Hurtubise forgot everything. He forgot his fears and his anxieties and he lost himself in the race.

He pushed his foot down on the accelerator and gripped the steering wheel as tightly as he could with his mangled hands. He charged around that track, losing himself in concentration. At the 65th mile Jim charged to the front of the pack. The crowd cheered its appreciation and admiration for a man whose determination was overshadowed only by his courage.

He pushed on, the crowd cheering and shouting its encouragement. He led at the 100th mile. He led at the 150th mile. He led at the 200th mile. And he led at the 249th mile. Now he could not be beaten. He was two

miles ahead of the field, and he pounded down the homestretch and came across the finish line a winner, the crowd's
roar exploding in his ears.

They went wild for Jim Hurtubise that day. They
cheered him and embraced him in their adulation. As he
pulled off the track he slowly passed the grandstand and
headed for victory lane, waving a mutilated hand to the
crowd in grateful appreciation.

Jim Hurtubise had come back . . . all the way back . . .
and nobody, in any sport, ever had it any harder or deserved
it any more.

JACKIE ROBINSON

"Do you think you've got the guts to play the game?"

He pushed the chair back and stood up, slowly circling to the front of the mahogany desk. His eyes were ablaze, peering out through horn-rimmed glasses under two black, bushy eyebrows. His face was in a scowling rage as his bulky, powerful body lumbered toward the young Negro, standing motionless before him. He dug an elbow into the Negro's ribs and his voice was like a rumble of thunder.

"What do you think you're doing?" he roared fiercely. "Get out of my way you dirty black ———."

Perspiration glistened on the young man's black face. His hands clenched into fists and he squeezed so hard the veins popped in his arms and his muscles tensed. There was hatred and fear in his dark eyes, and his lower lip quivered as he heard the man speak again.

"What do you do?" he asked, this time his voice less thunderous.

When the young Negro spoke, his voice was husky and stammering with emotion.

"Mr. Rickey," Jackie Robinson said, "do you want a ballplayer who's afraid to fight back?"

The old man growled his answer. "I want a ballplayer with guts enough *not* to fight back."

Rickey turned away, paced the floor, then quickly turned back. "You've got to do this job with base hits and stolen bases and fielding ground balls, Jackie. Nothing else."

It went on like this for three hours, the old man playing the role of various individuals, setting up hypothetical yet realistic situations. He was a southern hotel clerk denying the young man a room; he was the owner of a restaurant whose doors were closed to a hungry Robinson; he was a manager refusing Jackie admission to an imaginary movie house; he was a fan hurling insults and threats at the Negro from the safety of a seat in the grandstands.

"Now," he bellowed, "I'm playing against you in the World Series. I'm a hothead player. I want to win that game, so I go into you spikes high. But you don't give ground. You stand there and you jab the ball into my ribs and the umpire yells, 'Out!' I flare. All I see is your face

. . . that black face right on top of me. So I haul off and I punch you right in the cheek . . ." And he swung his huge fist through the air, barely missing the black, sweating face, which did not move. "What do you do?" Rickey demanded with a roar.

The young man seemed to tremble, to clench his fists, to breathe deeply. Then he answered in a whisper. "Mr. Rickey," he said, "I've got two cheeks . . . is that it?"

That was it. That was exactly it. Branch Rickey had found his man. He had been searching for three years and he had finally found his man.

The idea of signing a Negro baseball player first came to Branch Rickey early in 1943. It came to him not out of any overwhelming desire to be a trailblazer, a great, modern emancipator. His reasoning was quite simple and quite practical; he was interested in developing the best team possible for the Brooklyn Dodgers. Branch Rickey was then, and always would be, a fantastic builder of ball clubs, years ahead of his competitors. Negroes had succeeded in sports wherever they got the chance—Jesse Owens in track and field, Joe Louis and Jack Johnson in boxing—why not Negroes in baseball? Certainly Rickey was aware of the sociological significance of the move he contemplated, but he was motivated less by history than by the desire to win baseball games in Brooklyn. Neither was it, as many of his severest critics charged, a publicity stunt to revive interest in baseball that had waned during World War II; nor was it an attempt to hire "cheap labor." Rickey knew there would be such charges, he anticipated them, yet he went ahead with the plan, a plan so unconventional that it took great foresight and extreme moral courage to put it into practice.

Branch Rickey had long been aware of the struggle of the black man in America. He had championed the cause of civil rights and the equality of man from the time he coached baseball at the University of Michigan in 1908. On that Michigan team was a Negro player named Charley Thomas. On a trip to South Bend, Indiana, Thomas had been denied admittance to the hotel. Rickey persuaded the hotel clerk to allow Charley to stay in his room and the clerk agreed, provided Thomas did not sign the register and remained out of sight.

Later, Charley Thomas sat on a bed in Rickey's room, his head down, wringing his hands between his knees. When he looked up, there were tears in his eyes.

"What's the matter, Tommy?" Rickey asked.

"It's these," Charley Thomas said, holding up his hands. "It's my skin, my hands. They're black. If they were white, I wouldn't be any different from anybody else."

"Tommy," Rickey said softly, "the day will come when they won't have to be white."

The day came forty years later. It came for Charley Thomas and for all the Charley Thomases, and it came in the form of a muscular young man named Jackie Robinson.

Rickey knew that not just anyone could become the first Negro in organized baseball. He naturally had to be an outstanding player, one so good that he would not only make the major leagues, but would be a star in the majors. And that was not all. He had to be an outstanding person. He had to be kind, decent, intelligent and clean-living. And he had to have courage. He had to have the kind of courage that would make him stand up to the insults and taunts that no human being should have to endure. He had to want to do this thing more than anything else in the world. He had to want to do it at the risk of everything . . . even his life.

Rickey sent his best men into the field to scout the Negro leagues on the pretense they were looking for players for a proposed team, the Brooklyn Brown Dodgers, to represent Brooklyn in a new Negro league. They sent in reports and Rickey sifted through them carefully. Always he came back to the same name.

Jack Roosevelt Robinson had been born in Cairo, Georgia, to sharecropper parents. A few years later the family moved to California and, as a boy, Jackie sold newspapers on the streets of Pasadena to help support his family. He developed an all-consuming love for sports . . . all sports. In high school he excelled in basketball, baseball, football and track and field. But at UCLA he received his greatest acclaim as a football player.

World War II intervened before Jackie could get his degree and he was drafted. He entered the Army as a private, rose through the ranks and was discharged a second lieutenant. He joined the Kansas City Monarchs, a Negro baseball team. The reports Branch Rickey kept getting on the Monarchs' shortstop convinced him that Jackie Robinson was his man. He sent Clyde Sukeforth to get Robinson and bring him back to Brooklyn.

Sukeforth found Robinson in Chicago, playing against the Chicago American Giants in Comiskey Park on a blistering hot August afternoon in 1945. Before the game, Sukeforth, a meek, slim, little man, introduced himself to Robinson. "I'm Clyde Sukeforth," he said. "I represent the Brooklyn Dodgers' organization. I came out here to see you play."

Robinson was polite, but neither pleased nor impressed. People were always coming up to him and saying

they represented this or that. It got to be a joke among the
Monarchs. They kidded about it all the time, about someday
getting a chance to play in the major leagues. They talked
about it like people talk about winning the Irish sweepstakes, like some remote and impossible dream.

Jackie forgot all about Clyde Sukeforth during the
game, convinced he would never see the little fellow again.
But, when he had showered and dressed and walked out the
clubhouse door, there he was again, the same meek little
man, the same pleasant smile on his face, the same soft-
spoken voice.

"Mr. Rickey would like to see you in Brooklyn," Sukeforth said. Jackie was skeptical. Why would Mr. Rickey
want to see him?

Jackie had had the dream, too. He had more than that,
he had had a major league tryout. The Red Sox had invited
him and two other Negro players to Boston just that spring.
They worked out and they left, and they never heard from
the Red Sox again. People like Jackie Robinson don't hit
the Irish Sweepstakes. But, somehow, possibly because he
was a bigger dreamer than the others, possibly because he
believed in himself and in his fellow man, somehow Jackie
Robinson had an idea this was going to be different.

"Do you know why you were brought here?" Rickey
said from behind the mahogany desk in his plush office in
Brooklyn.

"Not exactly," Robinson admitted. "I heard something
about a colored team in Brooklyn. Is that it?"

"No," Rickey thundered, "that isn't it. You were
brought here, Jackie, to play for the Brooklyn organization.
Perhaps Montreal to start with, and after that . . ."

The words exploded in Jackie's ears. "Play for the Brooklyn organization. . . ." Could it be true? Could he have heard correctly?

". . . And after that you'll have a chance with the Brooklyn Dodgers. I want to win pennants and we need ballplayers, good ballplayers. Do you think you can make it? Do you think you can make good in organized baseball?"

"If I got the chance," Robinson said, haltingly.

"I want to give you that chance, but it will take a lot of courage. Do you think you've got the guts to play the game? They'll throw at your head. They'll insult you. They'll fight you. They'll call you every dirty name they can think of just to make it hard on you. It won't be easy."

"It won't be easy," Rickey had said. That was a gross understatement.

The announcement was made on October 23, 1945, in Montreal. Jackie Robinson had signed a contract to play for the Montreal Royals of the International League. The news was greeted with the expected mixed reaction from the press, fans and baseball officials. It was hailed in some quarters as a great step forward and was attacked in others as a cheap publicity stunt, one that very likely could have violent and unpleasant repercussions.

All the words written and all the words spoken could neither help nor hinder Jackie. All the encouragement and all the warnings meant little. This was his fight and he had to go out and win it by himself, on the field, in hotels, in restaurants.

He did not have to wait long for his first challenge. The Royals trained at Daytona Beach, Florida, but before opening camp they held a week of early drills at nearby

Sanford. So it was Sanford, Florida, where Robinson started his life in professional baseball. And it was Sanford which set the pattern that was to follow Jackie for the next few years. After two days the city's civic leaders demanded that Robinson leave town, and for the first time Jackie Robinson turned his cheek. He left.

A few weeks later the Royals had an exhibition game scheduled against the Jersey City Giants in Jacksonville, Florida. They made the ninety-mile trip by bus, and when they arrived at the park they found the gates locked. "The game's been called off," said a park attendant. "The Bureau of Recreation won't let you play because you've got colored boys on your team." Again Jackie turned his cheek.

Soon after there was another exhibition game against Indianapolis at Deland, Florida, and this time the game got off on schedule. But, in the first inning, Robinson got on base and came around to score, sliding into home with a cloud of dust. When the dust cleared, a local policeman was looking down into Jackie's face, hate in his eyes.

"Get off the field right now," the policeman ordered, "or I'm putting you in jail." Then he turned to Clay Hopper, the Montreal manager. "We ain't havin' Nigras mix with white boys in this town," he said. "Now, you tell that Nigra ah said to git." Robinson got.

One of the ironies of that first year in organized baseball was that he should have been assigned to play for a team whose manager came from Mississippi. It was an unusual coincidence. But was it a coincidence? Branch Rickey was too cunning, too careful to have overlooked that one little fact. It was part of the overall, well thought-out plan. If Jackie was the ballplayer and the man Rickey believed him to be, he would soon have Clay Hopper as his biggest booster. What better impetus for the project than to have a manager from Mississippi openly praise a Negro ball-player?

Hopper was an unwilling foil for Rickey's design. He never said he liked the idea of having Robinson on his team, and he never said he did not. He said nothing. He merely followed orders and went about his business, which was to win the pennant in the International League and develop ballplayers for the Brooklyn Dodgers.

His first spring training happily behind him, Jackie headed north for his debut in professional baseball.

There were more than 35,000 people in Roosevelt Stadium, Jersey City, that April 14, 1946. It was a strange crowd, mostly kids let out of school for opening day ceremonies, and they cheered loudly for the home team. But there was a burst of applause when the public address announcer blared in the first inning, "Now batting for Montreal . . . Jackie Robinson."

A wave of fear mixed with excitement came over Jackie as he stepped into the batter's box to await his first pitch in professional baseball. Would it be aimed at his head?

It was a ball . . . high but not tight. He worked the count to 3–2. Then he hit a weak ground ball to the shortstop and his knees trembled as he ran to first base.

He came to bat again with two men on base in the second inning. This time his bat met the ball solidly and the ball was a white dart, streaking out to left field where it disappeared over the fence. His first hit as a professional and it was a home run! He practically soared around the bases, and as he crossed home plate he exulted in the warmth of the crowd's cheering and the friendly congratulatory hand-shakes of his teammates.

When the game was over he trudged wearily to the dressing room and soaked himself in a warm shower. He had slammed four hits in five times at bat, hit a home run, had batted in four runs, stolen two bases, scored four runs and played a major part in the 14–1 victory.

The year was not without its distasteful incidents, how-ever. There were beanballs and there was name-calling. There were threats and insults. In Syracuse a player tossed a black cat on the field and shouted: "Hey, Robinson. Here's one of your relatives." In Baltimore players and fans cursed him and intimidated him, but always Jackie heeded Mr. Rickey's advice. He turned the other cheek.

Montreal won everything that year—the International League championship and the Little World Series—and Jackie was batting champion of the league with a .349 average. And he was the league's Rookie of the Year.

Speculation mounted that Robinson would certainly be called up to the Dodgers in 1947, but Rickey remained noncommital. Wisely, he arranged to have the Montreal and Brooklyn teams train together at Havana. This had a threefold purpose: it avoided a repetition of the kind of Florida hospitality Robinson had received in 1946; it gave the Dodger players an opportunity to play with the Negro Robinson and get to know him better; it delayed the neces-sity of an announcement concerning the disposition of Robinson's contract, since both minor leaguers and major leaguers were training together. Actually, Rickey had made up his mind, but the time was not right to announce it. He made up his mind immediately after the 1946 season, during organizational meetings which the Dodgers held in their Brooklyn offices with scouts, coaches and minor league managers. During the entire season Clay Hopper had not volunteered one bit of information on Robinson as man or athlete. Nothing good and nothing bad.

At one of the meetings Robinson's name came up and Rickey expressed doubt about Jackie's chances of making it with the Dodgers in 1947. "Oh, he did all right at Montreal," Rickey said, "but how do we know he'll hit big league pitching? And what about his off-field activities? How do we know he won't . . . well, get out of hand?"

The bait was set and Hopper took it. "Mistah Rickey, suh," he said, "you don't have to worry none about that boy. He's the greatest competitor ah ever saw and what's more, he's a gentleman."

Rickey had his answer, but he moved slowly. At Havana he took the first step. The Dodgers were set at second base with Eddie Stanky, but they were desperately in need of a first baseman. He ordered a first baseman's mitt delivered to Robinson. Jackie was puzzled as he took the glove and began to work out at a position he had never played.

Robinson was still the property of Montreal when the Royals and Dodgers arrived in Brooklyn on April 8 to play their traditional three-game pre-season exhibition series.

In the third game, while Jackie was down on the field playing first base in a Montreal uniform, a Dodger employee upstairs in the press box was tacking a short, inconspicuous notice on the bulletin board. It said simply:

Brooklyn announces the purchase of the contract of Jackie Roosevelt Robinson from Montreal. He will report immediately. Branch Rickey.

Becoming a Dodger player was easy. A note on a bulletin board, a routine change in his contract and a walk across the hall from the visitor's clubhouse to the home team's clubhouse after the game. Gaining acceptance as a Dodger was not quite that easy. Sensing the inevitable and determined not to play on the same team with a colored man, a group of Dodger players signed a petition that spring announcing their unwillingness to accept Robinson as a teammate. Rickey became aware of the petition and summoned each man, individually, to his office.

Some backed down when confronted by the stern old man and agreed to play with Robinson. Others stubbornly refused, but conceded they had little choice, although they preferred to be traded. Some were traded, but others were not. By the end of the season, those who remained accepted Robinson not only as a teammate, but as a friend.

Watching the abuse Jackie had to endure, it was impossible not to sympathize with him and to admire his strength and courage. The situation would have tested anyone's fortitude under normal conditions—trying to break in as a major leaguer in the middle of a tough pennant fight and playing a brand new position. For Robinson it required superhuman courage.

It was not easy. In some cities he could not stay at the same hotel as the rest of the team, he could not eat at the same restaurants as the rest of the team. There were pitches thrown at his head; vicious slurs and insults; anonymous threats of harm to him, his wife and son; flying spikes, and extra-hard tags with a baseball in the ribs. The Philadelphia Phillies were particularly vicious in their insults and name-calling. So vicious, in fact, that baseball commissioner Happy Chandler had to intercede and demand they put a stop to it.

On May 6 of his rookie year, the Dodgers were to play their first game against the St. Louis Cardinals. Several members of the Cardinals had secretly decided the game would never be played. They planned to strike if the Dodgers insisted on using Robinson against them. The plot, which ultimately would include players in the entire league, was exposed when it came to the attention of Ford C. Frick, then president of the National League. He acted with haste, issuing an ultimatum to ringleaders of the proposed strike.

"If you do this," Frick warned, "you will be suspended from the league. You will find that the friends you think you have in the press box will not support you, that you will be outcasts. I do not care if half the league strikes. All will be suspended. This is the United States of America and one citizen has as much right to play as any other."

The strike was cancelled. The game was played. Frick's ultimatum was a noble step and had as much as anything to do with guaranteeing the success of Jackie Robinson's mission.

As the season wore on, Robinson earned increasing respect from opponents and teammates, not out of sympathy or understanding for his battle, but for the only reason a ballplayer should be judged—for his work on the field. He batted .296, led the league in stolen bases with 29, had 12 home runs, 48 RBI's, was second in runs scored with 125 and was named the National League's Rookie of the Year. The Dodgers won the pennant in 1947, and who among them could say they would have won it without their rookie first baseman?

His first year was over. It had been painful, trying, difficult and frustrating. But it was also rewarding and joyous, because it was now over and he had accomplished the first step of this very important mission. As Branch Rickey said, "Here was a man whose wounds you could not feel or share."

But Jackie Robinson was never alone in his fight for acceptance. He had Branch Rickey for counsel; he had his wife Rachel for strength; he had coach Clyde Sukeforth for companionship and guidance, and, on the field, he had Pee Wee Reese.

There was one day in that first season when it had been particularly bad for Jackie. Players from the other team tore into him, physically and orally. Vile insults . . . vicious slurs . . . inhuman attacks on the young man who could not fight back. And when it had gotten completely out of hand; when it had become so unbearable it seemed Jackie would crack, that he would undo all the good he had done and fight back; when it seemed he could take it no longer, Pee Wee Reese jogged over to him from shortstop. He talked to him pleasantly and he put his arm, gently, on Robinson's shoulder. Press photographers sent the picture all around the country—the picture of Pee Wee Reese, who is from Louisville, Kentucky, telling the world, "I do not see the color of this man's face, I see only that the name on the front of his uniform is the same as the name on mine."

Two years later Jackie Robinson was the most celebrated player in the game. He led the league with a .342 batting average and 37 stolen bases. He hit 16 home runs and batted in 124 runs, and he was named the National League's Most Valuable Player.

Then it was 1950 and everything changed for him. It had been agreed between Robinson and Rickey that for three years he would take whatever was handed out. He would keep quiet, he would grit his teeth, he would turn his other cheek and take it.

Jackie's answer to other men's hate was to play even harder, as in this characteristic steal of home plate.

United Press International Photo

Now it was the fourth year and Jackie, now the Dodgers' regular second baseman, was free from his bondage of silence; he was free to fight back. If the situation demanded fists, he was free to use them. But most often he answered the ignorance of bigotry with base hits and stolen bases. He became the most daring, most exciting, most fiercely competitive player in the game. He became the leader of the great Dodger teams of the Fifties.

He did many great things on the ballfield in the six years that followed, but the one that is most remembered, the one that most characterized the competitive fire of the man, happened on the last day of the 1951 season. The Dodgers had dissipated a $13\frac{1}{2}$ game lead in August and, as they came down to the final day, they were tied for first place with the New York Giants. The Dodgers were in the midst of their game in Philadelphia when they saw on the scoreboard that the Giants had won in New York. A victory over the Phillies was imperative for the Dodgers to stay alive in the pennant race.

It came down to the bottom of the twelfth inning of a tie game. The Phillies loaded the bases with two out. Eddie Waitkus was the batter, and he smashed a blazing line drive just to the right of second base. Jackie dived for the ball, grabbing it just as it was about to go into center field. As he did, he fell heavily to the ground, his elbows digging into the pit of his stomach, knocking the wind from him. He had made the game-saving catch, but he lay on the ground writhing and gasping for breath.

Somehow he managed to hobble to the dugout where he sat slumped on the bench, completely exhausted. His face was a mask of weariness and pain as the trainer held a piece of ammonia-soaked cotton under his nose.

The Dodgers failed to score in their half of the thirteenth, and now they were to take the field for the last half of the inning. Pee Wee Reese led his teammates onto the field. At the top of the dugout steps Reese stopped and turned back to the dugout, where Robinson still slumped, too weary and too hurt to move.

"Push him up here, Doc," Reese shouted. "He'll be all right once he gets out on the field."

It was, in its way, a tribute to Robinson's courage and determination. And Reese was right—Jackie was all right. In the fourteenth inning he hit a home run, and the Dodgers went into a play-off with the Giants.

It is unfortunate that Jackie Robinson came to baseball too late. He was 28 years old when he joined the Brooklyn Dodgers. He played ten years, and he had a lifetime batting average of .311 under the most trying conditions any athlete has ever experienced. He might have played fifteen or twenty years and set unapproachable records if he had been given the chance to play earlier. He retired after the 1956 season and, in 1961, was elected to baseball's Hall of Fame.

There is no end to the Jackie Robinson story; there is only a beginning and a middle. His contribution to baseball lives on and will never die. It lives with Willie Mays, Frank Robinson, Hank Aaron, Maury Wills, Roberto Clemente, Tony Oliva, Richie Allen and hundreds of others who have come and gone and are still to come. Men who might have never been given the chance had it not been for one man's courage and will to succeed.

JERRY KRAMER

"Somebody wants to know if you're dead. What shall I tell him?"

Little Jerry Kramer, five years old and no more mischievous than any boy his age, picked up the axe and followed his mother outside. Jerry liked to help with the chores on the family farm in Jordan, Montana. He liked to milk the cows, feed the pigs and pitch hay, but the thing he liked best of all was chopping wood. As little as he was,

Jerry could handle an axe quite capably, and his mother permitted him to help her chop wood for the fire. In fact, she welcomed his help. How else was a boy to learn life's responsibilities?

Jerry always felt very proud and grown up when his mother said, as she did this day, "Jerry, let's go out and chop some firewood."

He grabbed his axe and followed his mother outside to the woodshed, where a pile of logs lay waiting to be chopped into small pieces. He lifted his axe, but he did not have a secure grip, and as he got it over his head, the axe slipped from his hands and the blade caught him on the chin and neck. Blood gushed furiously, splashing down his shirt.

His mother scooped Jerry in her arms and rushed him to the hospital where he was put under emergency surgery. Doctors worked for hours to save his life, and they said he was a very lucky boy. The blade of the axe missed hitting his throat by less than an inch. He would carry a five-inch scar on his neck for the rest of his life, but he would live and be good as new.

Jerry Kramer, 16 years old and full of the fun and adventure of most teenage farmboys, liked to hunt. His grandfather often let him borrow his old double-barrel shotgun, the one with the exposed hammer.

It was a Saturday in November, and Jerry and a few of his friends had arranged to go hunting. They hoped to get a pheasant or a duck for Thanksgiving Day dinner. They had planned to meet by the big rock at nine and, as usual, Jerry was the first to arrive. He climbed on the rock and sat there to wait for his friends, resting grandpa's old shot-

gun next to him. He began peeling pieces of moss off the
rock and rolling them down the side of the rock. One piece
would not roll, so he picked up the old shotgun to shove the
piece of moss down the side of the rock. As he did so, the
rock tripped the hammer and the gun exploded.

Blood poured down Jerry's right arm and, just at that
moment, a friend arrived. "I shot myself," Jerry said. "I
think we'd better get some help."

The nearest house was across a field more than one
hundred yards away, but Jerry and his friend ran all the
way and asked for help. Within minutes Doc Neil Wendle
arrived. He quickly rushed Jerry to the hospital, where he
found Jerry's right arm practically shattered. Ligaments
and muscles were hanging out; the flesh was rolled up the
underside of his arm all the way to the elbow, where it
came together with the material from his sweater, the wad-
dings of the shotgun shells, dirt and other foreign sub-
stances. But once again, Jerry was lucky. His right side had
pained him so much from the seventeen imbedded shotgun
pellets that he hardly thought about the arm. If he had, he
might have wiped away the blood. Instead, the blood flowed
freely, serving as a cleansing agent and washing away all
the dirt in the wound.

For seven days Jerry remained on the critical list. He
remembers his parents coming to visit him one night. He
was doped with medication, but he was conscious and he
could see as if in a fog. He could make out the voices of
his parents and Doc Wendle whispering to them, and he
saw Doc take out a pencil and touch his arm just below the
elbow. Even in his stupor Jerry knew what Doc Wendle was
saying, and it sent a chilling fear rushing right through

him. Doc Wendle was indicating where he would cut when
he amputated the arm.

By some miracle the arm began to improve almost
immediately, and the doctor decided it could be saved.
With the aid of skin grafts, Doc Wendle was able to restore
almost full use of the arm, although it has remained scarred
and withered for life. There is a groove running from the
elbow to the wrist that resembles the gutter in a bowling
alley, and the hand is locked in a semi-clutch. Part of the
circulation is cut off from the fingers, leaving them sensitive
to rapid temperature changes.

Jerry by that time was a star tackle on the football
team and a star track man at Sand Point High in Sand
Point, Idaho, where his family had moved some years before. He knew the arm injury would not stop him from
playing football. Earlier in the season he backed into a
lathe in woodworking class, cutting a hunk of flesh out of
his hip, but he played football that night. Not even a withered arm could end his football days, but he knew he was
finished as a discus thrower. Instead, he switched to the
shot put the following spring and set a state record with a
throw of 51 feet, 10 inches.

Jerry Kramer, 17 years old and frisky as a young
colt, came home from swimming one summer afternoon
and found a calf running loose on the farm. He took out
after the calf, chasing it for half an hour. Just as he was
about to catch up with it, the calf's foot came down in the
middle of a rotten plank that had been torn off an old shed.
The plank splintered and a long, jagged piece shot up and
pierced Jerry where the leg joins the body. He pulled the
sliver out and went into the house to tell his father what
had happened.

Jerry's dad called Doc Wendle, who asked to see the boy in the hospital immediately. Unable to find anything, Doc sent Jerry home to rest. But the next day Jerry felt a stabbing pain in his back, like a knife digging into him. He went back to the hospital; X rays were taken and showed nothing. Still the pain persisted. Perplexed, Doc Wendle returned to the Kramer farm to search for the broken plank. He pieced it together and noticed a large chunk still missing. Since wood has the same density as tissue, it was possible a sliver still remained in Jerry's body, undetected by the X rays.

Jerry was rushed to a hospital in Spokane, Washington, seventy miles away, where more extensive examination revealed another piece of wood three-quarters of an inch wide and $7\frac{1}{2}$ inches long lodged in the back, just about to puncture the spine. The wood was removed, and three weeks later Jerry was playing football again.

Completing his senior year at Sand Point High, named to the all-state high school football team and awarded a scholarship to the University of Idaho, Jerry Kramer went out to celebrate his success one night with a friend. Returning home, his friend lost control of his car and it shot off the road into a ditch, throwing Jerry and the driver clear. The car rammed a tree and burst into flames, but Jerry and his friend walked away without a scratch.

Incredibly, though he had spent more time in hospitals than Ben Casey, Jerry had never been injured on the football field. In his junior year at Idaho the inevitable happened. He complained of a sharp pain in his neck, and X rays showed he had a chipped vertebra. He was sent for an operation to the familiar hospital in Spokane where, by now, he was on a first-name basis with the doctors. They said they would fix him up and only a small scar would remain. The scar is six inches long, running a jagged route up his back to his neck. It looks like a zipper.

Miraculously, Jerry managed to get through his senior year without incident. He made the East-West Shrine Game and was drafted on the fourth round by the Green Bay Packers.

The once proud, powerful and tradition-steeped Packers had fallen on evil times. It had been years since they were in contention for the league championship, and in 1957 they had finished sixth in their division. But they had begun a rebuilding program that would hopefully carry them back to the top of the National Football League. In the past two years they had drafted Paul Hornung, Bart Starr, Forrest Gregg, Hank Gremminger and Max McGee.

In 1958 their first draft choice was Dan Currie, a linebacker from Michigan State. Second was Jim Taylor, a fullback from LSU, and third was Ray Nitschke, a linebacker from Illinois. Their fourth draft choice was Jerry Kramer, a tackle from the University of Idaho. Their most important addition was to come the following year when Vince Lombardi, the scholarly-looking, tough-talking, imaginative offensive coach of the New York Giants was brought in as head coach.

Jerry Kramer's first year in professional football was one of shocking indoctrination, of painful but vital experience. Shifted from tackle to guard and used only on offense, Jerry started learning the facts of NFL life in a hurry from some of the meanest, roughest, cruelest, cleverest customers in the business. And he has the scars to prove it . . . both mental and physical.

In one game against the Baltimore Colts, Kramer was matched with mean and mammoth Artie Donovan, 280 pounds of granite with a heart to match. Donovan knew all the tricks in the pro lineman's book, and he used every one of them, with a few variations of his own. Kramer took the beating of his life that day, but he learned a valuable lesson. "When the game was over," he recalls, "and the Colts were walking off the field, it was all I could do to keep from running across the field and putting a block on that Donovan just to see how it would feel."

But Jerry Kramer learned his lessons well, and two years later he was being hailed as one of the finest offensive guards in the game. With Fuzzy Thurston at the other guard, the Packers had two of the fiercest, most effective blockers in the game. These men were absolutely vital for the type of running game Lombardi used, for 85 percent of the time one of the guards pulled out to lead the blocking. Lombardi had put the Packers back on top of the violent world of professional football that year, and Jerry Kramer had as much to do with it as anyone; his devastating blocks had often cleared paths for Jim Taylor and Paul Hornung.

One day a reporter asked Kramer: "How does it make you feel when you and Thurston do all the heavy work leading those plays and Hornung and Taylor get all the credit?"

"That's all right," Jerry replied. "As long as they keep taking those pictures of Hornung and Taylor scoring, Fuzzy and I will be in there somewhere."

Kramer's work did not go unnoticed; it was appreciated where it counts . . . by coach Lombardi. "Some think he's the greatest blocker in the game," Lombardi said, lead-

ing to the feeling that the coach was one of those who
thought so.

But in the middle of that great 1960 season, in a game
against the Los Angeles Rams, Kramer put a trap block on
large Lamar Lundy. The next thing Kramer knew, he could
no longer remember the plays. Before each play he had to
ask Jim Ringo and Forrest Gregg which man he had to
block. At first they thought it was a joke, but they soon
realized what had happened: Kramer was dazed and in a
stupor, playing on instinct alone like a fighter out on his
feet.

After the game Kramer complained of a dot flashing
in his right eye, but he dismissed it. Five games later he
realized he was having trouble seeing out of his right eye,
but he kept it a secret. The Packers had won the Western
Division title and were to meet the Philadelphia Eagles for
the NFL championship and, as Kramer later explained,
"How often does a guy get a chance to play in a championship game?"

The Packers lost the game, and Kramer returned to
Green Bay for an examination of his right eye. It was
diagnosed as a detached retina and he underwent a delicate
operation to save the sight in his eye. Nine days later he
was playing golf.

Although he played the last half of the season with a
detached retina and impaired vision in one eye, Jerry was
named to the all-pro team and he eagerly looked forward
to the start of the 1961 season. He had come a long way
in just three years. He had perfected the intricate play of
the offensive guard under the complex running game of
Vince Lombardi. He had learned enough to stand up to the

giant tackles and ends who populated professional football. But he had not shaken the injury jinx.

It struck again early in the 1961 season in a game against the Minnesota Vikings. He was caught on a pickoff play and suffered a severe fracture of the tibia, the main bone in the leg, which became separated from his ankle. The doctors put a bolt in the ankle to hold the bone in place, and they speculated that it might mean the end of Jerry's career. They did not know Jerry Kramer. An axe could not stop him. A shotgun blast could not stop him. He would shake off a mere broken bone in no time.

"Kramer," coach Lombardi once said, "has the perfect devil-may-care attitude it takes to play this game. He not only ignores the small hurts, but the big ones, too."

He ignored the broken leg and he was playing again in 1962. And there never was a year like that. He made the all-pro team again, and when Paul Hornung was hurt in mid-season, Jerry took over as the team's place kicker although he had not kicked since his senior year at Idaho. He kicked 9 field goals and 38 extra points as the Packers won the Western Division title and went to New York to play the Giants for the World Championship.

It was cold and windy in Yankee Stadium that December day in 1962, but Jerry Kramer kicked a 26-yard field goal for the first score in the game. Jim Taylor's seven-yard touchdown run and Kramer's extra point made it 10–0 at the half. In the second half the Giants came back. They scored a touchdown to make it 10–7, but Kramer kicked a 29-yard field goal for a six-point lead, and then he kicked one from 30 yards out. That was all the scoring there was. The Green Bay Packers were world champions!

Trouble struck Green Bay in 1963. Paul Hornung, the golden boy of football, was suspended for betting on games. Kramer took over as the team's place kicker and set a Green Bay record with 43 extra points and 16 field goals for a total of 91 points. The Packers did not miss Hornung's kicking, but they missed his running and blocking, and they lost the Western Division title to the Chicago Bears.

Hornung was back in 1964, and it was going to be a big year for the Green Bay Packers. You could tell it was going to be a big year from the attitude of the coaches and players in training camp. It was all business and hard work in camp that summer, and Jerry Kramer could not remember ever having worked so hard. Coach said he might have to do the place kicking again. Paul would be rusty and he would be under enough pressure just running and blocking —it would be unfair to overload him. And so Jerry worked harder than ever to perfect his blocking and his kicking.

And then it was August, and just as the team was ready to break camp it hit him: cold chills, high fever and sharp, shooting pains in his stomach that doubled Jerry up in agony. At first he dismissed it. "Been working too hard," he said. "I've got a bug, that's all. I'll be all right."

But he was not all right. He played the first game of the season, but he did not play well. He could no longer hide his illness. He still had the pains in his stomach, the fever persisted and he was rapidly losing weight. They sent him back to St. Vincent's Hospital in Green Bay for exploratory surgery. Doctors found and removed a tumor the size of a grapefruit from his stomach. Further surgery was required, and Jerry was sent to the Mayo Clinic in Rochester, Minnesota, for a second operation . . . then a third. While he was still on the operating table after his third

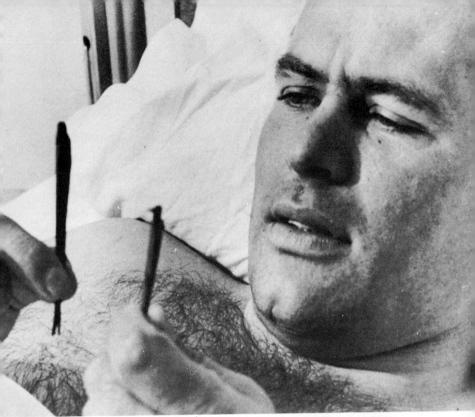

Jerry inspects two of the three wooden "splinters" which were removed from his intestine.

operation, the doctor examined him and suggested another operation immediately. He had developed pneumonia and high fever, but fifteen minutes after the third operation, he had his fourth.

By now the word had spread through the pro football grapevine that Jerry Kramer was dying of stomach cancer. The word even reached Jerry Kramer. He was quite sure it was untrue because the doctors told him the tumor had been non-malignant, but how could he be positive they were

telling him the truth? How did he know they were not holding back on him, sparing him the awful news?

He still was not feeling right, and a fifth operation was
scheduled at St. Vincent's. It was then that they found the
source of all his trouble. Lodged in his intestine were three
more slivers of wood from the time he chased the calf twelve
years before. He had been carrying them around in his intestine all those years. There was one piece of wood a half
inch wide, an eighth of an inch thick and four inches long,
plus two smaller pieces three and two inches long. They
had been there all the time, undetectable by X rays and
pressing against the wall of the intestine. Finally one of the
slivers had punctured the intestine, allowing bacteria to
escape into the bloodstream and eventually to reach the
liver. It caused a fungus growth known as actinomycosis.

Curious, Jerry looked the word up in a medical journal. The words practically leaped off the page at him ". . .
intestinal disorder that is uniformly fatal." Jerry Kramer
laughed. He was reading a 1950 journal.

Still the rumors persisted about him and one day, sitting in his doctor's office, the telephone rang. "Somebody
wants to know if you're dead," the doctor said. "What shall
I tell him?"

"Tell him," Kramer said with a smile, "I don't think
so, but I really can't be sure because I don't know what it's
like to be dead."

He went home and there were twenty more telephone
calls from people who were surprised to hear his voice.
He went to his barber for a haircut and when he entered, the
barber looked at him in disbelief. "I was just taking up a
collection to buy you flowers," the barber said. "Ten min-

utes ago you were a great guy. Now you're still the same
old bum."

After that there were three more operations to fix him
up completely, and when they were over, it was the summer
of 1965 and the Green Bay Packers were ready to leave for
training camp. Jerry Kramer vowed he would be there with
them. In his 29 years he had had 23 operations and more
than 500 stitches, but he was not through yet.

His weight had dropped to 210, 40 pounds below his
normal playing weight, but he was determined to play
football again. He telephoned coach Lombardi. "Look,
Jerry," Lombardi said, "I can't tell you not to come. I owe
you that much. But I have to tell you I'm not counting on
you."

It was not a yes but it was not a no, and that was
enough for Jerry. He was a month late arriving in camp.
His weight was now 225, but he was still 25 pounds too
light. Lombardi gave him little to do. He worked Jerry
with the kickers, but he would not work him with the offensive line. That Jerry had to do on his own. At night, when
practice was over, he would go out on the field alone and
work to get himself into playing condition.

In a month he had built himself back to 250 pounds.
He had regained his strength, but Lombardi still refused to
take chances, still refused to work him with the regulars,
still would not offer any encouragement. And who could
blame him? Here was a man who had just undergone eight
major operations in less than a year. Here was a man who
had been rumored dead. Here was a man whose tissues had
become so weak after seven operations that he developed
a hernia and had to have an eighth operation. It was un-

thinkable that he could ever play football . . . certainly not so soon. But it was not unthinkable to Jerry Kramer.

The week before the Packers' first exhibition game, Kramer went to Lombardi. "You've got to give me a chance, coach," he pleaded. "If I don't play now I'll never be ready. I feel great. I know I can do the job. Take a chance, what have you got to lose?"

Lombardi had nothing to lose and so he took a chance. He played Jerry Kramer at guard in that first exhibition game, and six weeks later, when the Packers opened the 1965 season in Pitt Stadium against the Pittsburgh Steelers, Jerry Kramer was in the starting lineup.

The 1965–1966 season was a great one for Jerry Kramer and for the Green Bay Packers. And it culminated on the morning of January 2, 1966, a bitter, cold and wet day in Green Bay, Wisconsin. Outside 50,852 fans huddled under blankets and storm coats, waiting for their beloved Packers to take on the Cleveland Browns for the championship of the National Football League. It had snowed during the night and the workmen were up early to clear the field and push the blanket of white to the sidelines, leaving the field soft and wet.

In the Green Bay dressing room, the green and gold uniformed Packers sat nervously in front of their lockers. In ten minutes they would charge out onto the field for the biggest game many of them would ever play.

Jerry Kramer's stomach jumped nervously. He had been through this before, but somehow this seemed like the first time. He looked around the room. He saw Jim Taylor . . . Paul Hornung . . . Willie Davis . . . Fuzzy Thurston . . . Ray Nitschke . . . Henry Jordan . . . and he wondered if they felt the way he did.

Coach Lombardi was in the center of the room, looking through horn-rimmed glasses and talking in that soft but gruff way of his. He was directing his remarks to Bart Starr, the quarterback. "The field is muddy," Lombardi was saying. "We may not be able to use our running game as much as we usually do. We may have to throw the ball a lot. . . ."

He was finished. They jumped to their feet with a shout and clomped onto the field. The voices of 50,000 fans roared with approval, imploring them to "Beat the Browns!"

The first half was a hard, bruising battle. Unable to move on the ground, the Packers had scored first when Starr threw 47 yards to Carroll Dale. He made a sensational catch and scored easily when Cleveland defenders Ross Fichtner and Larry Benz slipped in the mud. The extra point made it 7–0. Minutes later, Cleveland quarterback Frank Ryan completed three consecutive passes, the last one to Gary Collins for a touchdown. A bad pass from center spoiled Lou Groza's extra point try and the Packers led, 7–6. Both teams failed to move the ball and each settled for a pair of field goals. As they went off the field at halftime, the Packers' held a precarious 13–12 lead.

In the third period the superior and stronger Packer line began wearing down the Browns' defense with short, rapid bursts like machine-gun fire. It was bruising, brutal, neanderthal football played in slime, and the invincible Packer linemen punished their opponents to a man.

The Packers had pushed to the Cleveland 13-yard line midway in the period. In the huddle Jerry Kramer heard Bart Starr call a play and, instinctively, he went over the play in his mind, making certain he knew what his assignment was. It was to be a handoff to Hornung and a sweep left . . . a very difficult play considering the condition of the field. Kramer was to pull out of the line and lead Hornung downfield, picking up either the halfback or the safety. It was a play the Packers had worked successfully on numerous occasions, but one that required precision blocking even under ideal conditions.

They snapped out of the huddle. Kramer moved quickly and confidently to the line of scrimmage, quickly checking his defensive opponent, Dick Modzelewski, with a furtive glance. He saw Ken Bowman, next to him, come over the ball, and he heard Bart Starr call his signals. Precisely at the snap of the ball, Kramer pulled back away from Modzelewski, pivoted and cut to his left. As he did, he could hear Hornung at his heels, and up ahead he could see Brown players dropping to the ground as the Packers did their usual great job of precision blocking.

Now they were inside the 10-yard line and they had daylight. As they reached the five, Kramer could see two white-shirted Browns coming up to meet the ball carrier. Jerry crouched a little lower and braced for the impact, throwing his body into those white shirts with all the force and power he could muster. He obliterated both of them with the devastating, crunching block that is his trademark. And as the three of them fell to the ground, Jerry could hear Hornung's footsteps pounding by into the end zone without so much as a hand being laid on him. And he could hear the crowd come alive with a deafening roar. He knew he had done his job. He had made the important block on what had been the big insurance play of the game. The Packers had an eight-point lead and they would not give that back. Not today.

The game ended 23–12. The Packers were once again World Champions. One by one the players squeezed through the horde of fans and down the runway into the corridor that led to the dressing room. Their uniforms were caked with mud and weariness lined their faces, but as they came into the dressing room, they shouted with joy and patted each other on the back. In their biggest game, in a sea of mud that limited their skills, the Packers had, once again, shown their toughness. They were champions again.

Jerry Kramer pushed his way into the room and headed for his locker. He sat down heavily, spent with emotional and physical exhaustion. One by one other players came to him to shake his hand, to pound his back, to shout "great blocking, Whale."

Now the television cameramen and radio and press reporters pushed into the room. They came to Kramer, their tape recorders and notebooks in hand, and they congratulated him and waited for him to say something . . . something they could record for posterity.

"I wasn't old enough in 1961 and 1962," he said. "I didn't know how much it meant then. Now I know." And, as he talked, in Jerry Kramer's eyes there was pain and exhaustion, happiness and tears.

BOB PETTIT

"He would practice and practice until he got it right."

"The greatest thing that ever happened to me is that when I first picked up a basketball I was terrible. If things come naturally, you may not bother to work at improving them and you can fall short of your potential."

The author of that statement is Bob Pettit, who retired
from professional basketball in 1965 after having scored
more points than any other player in the history of the
game. It is vivid proof of that ancient sports adage that
champions are made, not born. It is testimony to the belief
that a man can succeed by substituting hard work, desire
and determination for pure natural ability. It is an example
of what can be accomplished through sacrifice.

In truth, Bob Pettit was not without an inherent advantage, which came in the form of parental help. His
father was a robust, strapping 6'4", possessed of natural
athletic ability. His mother was 5'8" and she had four
brothers, all over six feet tall. Pettit's heritage was, unde-
niably, a vital factor in his success. But he was not born six
feet, nine inches tall—birth records in Baton Rouge, Louisiana, clearly state that on December 12, 1932, Mrs. Robert
E. Lee Pettit, Sr., gave birth to a nine-pound, one-ounce
boy. And he was not 6'9" when he entered Baton Rouge
High thirteen years later.

True, Pettit began to sprout as a teenager, but without
determination, hard work, courage and the stubborn re-
fusal to quit in the face of ridicule and failure, Bob Pettit
would have grown up to become the tallest bank teller in
Baton Rouge. With those qualities, he grew up to become
one of the greatest players the game of basketball has ever
known.

As a boy, Bob Pettit loved sports—all sports. He
played constantly and, like most boys, he played every
major sport, changing the game when the seasons changed.
His father, who was the sheriff of Baton Rouge, encouraged

Bob to play, but never pushed him toward basketball even though he himself had been a basketball player at Westminster College. Bob's dad made sure his boy always had all the athletic equipment he needed. The Pettits were not rich, but they lived comfortably in a big house and Bob was an only child. But he was not pampered.

Bob grew up tall and straight like a young sapling—and he was about as mobile. He was taller than most boys his age when he entered Baton Rouge High, and he was skinnier, too. At the age of thirteen he stood 5'7" and weighed only 118. "I had more of a figure than a build," he says. But his great love was football. He went out for the freshman football team, and a coach with either a great sense of humor or a terrible personnel problem put him at tackle.

In one game he was sent in to play right tackle on defense. Instead he lined up at left tackle, and on the next play the opponents went 65 yards for a touchdown right through the spot left vacant by the confused Pettit. That ended a football career that, if nothing else, had at least been different.

In baseball someone got the idea Bob should play second base. The first time a ball was hit to him it went right through his spindly legs. But Bob kept trying. He played baseball every day, but try as he might, he could not improve. Whenever the fellows chose sides for a game, he was always the last one picked. It did very little for his confidence. He was growing so fast he could not get accustomed to his body. He was awkward and frail, with about as much coordination as a telephone pole.

By the process of elimination, Bob had little choice but to concentrate on basketball. As a freshman he made the school's junior varsity, but he soon realized his function on the team was merely to fill out the bench. He played rarely, getting into a game only when the score was lopsided and the outcome no longer in doubt. After each game the players on the team would stand around under the shower rejoicing in victory or lamenting in defeat. Bob could take part neither in the joy nor the sorrow because he had made no contribution. After a winning game, when his teammates would ask one another how many points they scored, Bob pretended he did not hear. He hoped they would not ask him because he never scored a point. Not one point the entire season!

Once the team had a road game. They were to travel by bus fifteen miles north of Baton Rouge to the town of Zachary, Louisiana. Weeks before the scheduled trip, Bob began planning for the journey. Even if he would not get in the game, it made him feel like part of the team, like a professional athlete to be going on a road trip. He imagined himself riding in the bus and arriving at Zachary. The team would file out of the bus and he would hold his head up proudly as if he were the star of the team. The little kids would be standing there watching him, envying him, just as he did when he watched the Louisiana State University basketball team file out of its bus.

Finally the big day arrived and Bob rushed to school, unable to control his excitement. When he got there, he learned the bus had broken down and the trip would have to be made by automobile. But there was not enough room in the car for everyone, and the coach said some of the players would have to stay behind. There was room only for the first five players and the first two substitutes. Naturally, Pettit was left behind. He said he understood and it did not matter to him. He wished his teammates luck in the game in Zachary and he stood on the sidewalk, hurt and humiliated, watching the car pull away.

In his sophomore year Bob answered the call for tryouts for the varsity basketball team. He was one of seventeen who showed up at the tryout, but the coach had only twelve uniforms. When the day came to hand out the uniforms, Bob Pettit was one of the five who did not get one.

The pain of rejection cut deeply into the young boy. He hungered to wear the green and gold lettered athletic sweater of Baton Rouge High. Just as fierce was the competitive flame that burned within him. But it seemed Bob Pettit's athletic career had ended even before it started. He tried to tell himself he did not need the silly kid's game. He said there were more important things in life. But he knew he was only lying to himself.

It hurts to be rejected at the age of fourteen. It is the end of the world . . . if you accept it as such. Bob Pettit would not accept it. There was still a lot of fight left in him. He was consumed by a desire to play, a determination to win that green and gold sweater.

With time on his hands, Bob began to spend his afternoons at St. James Episcopal Church. He had always been active in church affairs, singing in the choir, taking up collections at Sunday services, serving as an altar boy. Soon the church became a haven for other high school basketball dropouts and the pastor, Mr. Philip Werlein, suggested the boys of St. James start a basketball team of their own. They could play games against boys from two other neighboring churches and, in time, they might even form their own three-team church league.

It seemed like a good idea. At least it would fulfill the need for competition that dwells in all young boys. The games in the three-team church league were organized mayhem. What went on on the basketball court of St. James was like nothing these boys had ever experienced. A lack of supervision, a lack of proper coaching, a lack of good officiating made it survival-of-the-strongest basketball. But although it was not Baton Rouge High, it did make Bob feel like part of a team. For the first time, he had a feeling of belonging.

With his interest in athletics reawakened and his desire to be the best player in his league rekindled, Bob started practicing at home. With a wire coat hanger he improvised a hoop which he hung over the garage door. Every chance he got he would shoot tennis balls at the hoop. Indoors, he would throw rolled-up paper into a wastebasket. His father was pleased with this sudden interest in basketball. "If it means that much to you," he said one day, "let's get some lumber and nails."

Together they erected a backboard and rim in the backyard. Bob's dad bought him a basketball, and the youngster began a routine which he followed religiously for the next seven years. He shot baskets by the hour.

He would arrive home from school at 3:30 and shoot baskets for two hours. Then he would do his lessons and

have his dinner, and at 7:30 he was out shooting baskets
again. When it got dark he took two lamps, put them on the
windowsill facing the backyard, and continued shooting
baskets until it was time to go to bed. Over the next seven
years he shot millions of baskets, and soon he began to
develop the familiar push shot that was to become his trademark years later. He improved steadily. He could throw
his push shot through the hoop from almost any distance
with amazing accuracy, and he became the leading scorer
on his church team. It still wasn't Baton Rouge High, but it
represented tremendous progress over the last few months.

Bob did not yet have strength, coordination or stamina.
His father suggested a program for building up his body
just as he had built up his ability to shoot a basketball. He
suggested rope-skipping and table tennis for coordination
and weight lifting for strength. Bob would take window
shade weights and do exercises to build up his arms. To
strengthen his legs, he would stand on the back steps, hold
on to the screen door and do calf raises.

When school ended, Bob prevailed upon his father to
send him to Camp Dudley, a boys' camp in Lake George,
New York. At Camp Dudley Bob did nothing but play basketball, ten hours a day, seven days a week for six weeks.
He could feel himself getting better and stronger, and he
could see himself growing taller.

By the time he entered his junior year, Pettit had
sprouted to 6'4". Again he went out for the varsity basketball team, and this time there was a uniform for him. Even
if he had not improved his play he still would have made
the team because he was by far the tallest boy trying out

for the squad. Naturally, he was put at center. All he had to do was simply stand around, block shots and take a few rebounds. But Bob surprised everyone with his tremendous improvement and his shooting accuracy. He was not a star, but he played regularly, averaging fourteen points a game and earning that precious green and gold lettered sweater. On the hottest days in May and June, Bob would go to school wearing his sweater. "People thought I was crazy," he later confided. "But I had worked too hard for that sweater to let it hang in the closet."

Things began to happen for Bob Pettit in his senior year. He had grown three more inches and he was full of confidence. His reputation also grew, and he began to get offers from colleges all over the country when he poured in 33 points in a game early in the season.

He missed nine games because of the mumps, but when he returned he led Baton Rouge High to an eighteen-game winning streak and the state championship. He averaged 19 points a game with a high of 41, and he was selected to play in the North-South All-America high school game in Murray, Kentucky. Fourteen colleges were bidding for his services when he graduated, but Bob never had any doubt as to which one he would choose. He had always harbored a secret dream to someday play basketball at Louisiana State University.

If things came hard for him in high school, they were ridiculously easy in college. He had grown to his full height of 6'9", and rarely did he come up against an opponent who was as tall. The Pettit career flourished at LSU. He set school records that still stand—50 points against Georgia, 45 against Georgia Tech, 60 against Louisiana College. He set the school scoring and rebounding record, was named on several All-America teams, was among the leading scorers in the country in each of his four varsity seasons and was selected as the number one draft choice of the Milwaukee (later St. Louis) Hawks.

Pettit found things not quite as easy in the National Basketball Association. He had come into the league full of confidence, loaded down with dozens of college records and a big reputation. But he was playing with men now, and he suddenly found he was no longer the biggest kid on his block. Others towered over him and he could no longer get by just with his height. The pro game was faster, tougher and rougher than any he had ever experienced, and it took many bumps and bruises for Pettit to make the grade. He learned the facts of NBA life in a hurry. In an exhibition game against the Minneapolis Lakers, he came face-to-face with such man mountains as George Mikan, 6'10" and 275 pounds, Clyde Lovelette, 6'9" and 245 pounds and Vern Mikkelsen, 6'7" and 255 pounds.

Rookie Pettit was assigned to guard Mikkelsen, one of the meanest, strongest men in the game. In the first half Bob took a merciless pounding from the veteran, and during the halftime break coach Red Holzman put it on the line for his rookie sensation. "Tell me, Pettit," he said, "do you like playing professional basketball?"

"Why, yes, Mr. Holzman," Pettit replied, puzzled. "I think it's fine. I'm having a real good time."

"Well, let me tell you something, boy," the coach exploded. "If you don't go out there and hit the first guy you see coming at you, I'm going to send you back to Baton Rouge tomorrow. The first guy who comes close to you in the second half I want you to hit with an elbow. You have to get a little aggressive or you'll never make it in the pros."

Somewhat frightened by Holzman's threats, Pettit went out in the second half and looked around for somebody to hit. He spotted Slater Martin, all 5'10", 165 pounds of him.

"There," he thought, "is my man."

On the first play of the half, Martin streaked by Pettit, who had taken the ball on the high post. Bob swung around, quickly sending his elbow flying. But Martin whizzed by so fast that Pettit missed him. Instead, he smashed Mikkelsen right in the chest with his elbow. Mikkelsen looked at Pettit menacingly, and Bob could feel the crimson rushing to his face as he looked for a hole in the floor in which to bury himself.

"Please excuse me, Mr. Mikkelsen," he said meekly.

But the meek do not inherit the NBA. Veterans look for and exploit any show of timidity, and Pettit soon learned he must get tough to survive. Another of his problems was learning a new position in the pros. He had played center in college, but he was not tall enough or strong enough for that position in the pros. He was shifted to forward and had to learn an entirely new style of play. He studied hard and he practiced hard, averaging three hours a day to perfect a jump shot and to improve his defense and rebounding. It did not come easy for him, but nobody ever worked harder than Bob Pettit.

"He had to learn the pro game from scratch," Holzman said. "He had to learn how to use his weight, how to block out, how to rebound off the offensive board, how to go off a screen. He would practice and practice until he got it right."

As a pro he applied the same dedication, the same desire for perfection, the same hunger to succeed that had transformed him from a spindly, awkward kid into the star of his high school team.

"What it is with me, I guess," Pettit has said, "is that as you go along in life and work hard, you reach new plateaus of accomplishment. With each plateau you reach, the demands upon you become greater. And your pride increases to meet the demands. You drive yourself harder than before. You can't afford negative thinking, so you always believe you'll win. You build an image of yourself that has nothing to do with ego—but it has to be satisfied. When I fall below what I think I can do, my belly growls and growls. Anytime I'm not playing up to my very best, I can count on a jolt of indigestion."

The spirit of competition and the overwhelming desire to succeed were so all-consuming in Pettit that he refused to submit to any setback, particularly a physical one. In his career he has had 125 stitches taken in his body.

In one game against the Boston Celtics, he was hit over the left eye by Tom Heinsohn just as the first half ended. The blood gushed from the cut as Bob was taken

off the floor and into the clubhouse, where he was attended
by Dr. Stan London.

"That's a deep cut, Bob," Dr. London said. "It will
take a lot of repair work. We'll have to call for an ambulance and have you taken to the hospital."

"Can't we delay the hospital thing until after the second half, Doc?" Pettit pleaded. "Can't you patch me up
good enough to hold me for another 25 minutes?"

Right there in the dressing room Dr. London took fourteen stitches in Bob's eyebrow and sent him out to start the
third period. He scored eighteen points in the half and the
Hawks won the game.

Another time he was slugged in the mouth by a stray
elbow. He left the floor, came back minutes later and finished the game with seventeen stitches in his mouth and jaw.

In 1957, Pettit's third season in the NBA, he was
leading a fast break when he tripped over Jim Loscutoff of
the Celtics and landed on his arm. He broke a metacarpal
bone in his right wrist, and it was feared he would be lost
for the season. Without their star the Hawks would certainly lose the division title which had seemed so close.
Pettit would not accept the inevitable. He asked the doctors
if they could devise some sort of cast which would permit
him to continue playing. They did. They came up with a
unique getup. It was turned in such a peculiar angle that
when Bob lifted his hand he was in a shooting position.
Bob missed only one game. And even though playing with
the hand in a cast that presented an inviting target to opposing hatchet men, he led the Hawks to the division title

and took Boston the full seven games for the league championship. What's more, he finished only 62 points behind Paul Arizin for the league scoring championship. In the play-offs he was by far the leading scorer with 298 points in ten games.

The following year he broke another bone in his shooting hand, this time near the thumb. Another playing-cast was designed, and Pettit entered the all-star game with his hand still in the cast.

"Don't take any chances, Bob," Hawk owner Ben Kerner instructed. "We've got a chance to go all the way this year, so please play it safe."

Asking Bob Pettit to take it easy in a basketball game is like asking pitcher Early Wynn, one of baseball's fiercest competitors, if he would allow his mother to take a toehold at the plate against him. "Mother," Wynn replied to the questioner, "was a pretty good hitter."

Pettit's answer to his boss was equally emphatic. He scored 28 points, an all-star record, took 26 rebounds and was voted the game's Most Valuable Player.

Playing with the broken bone for most of the season, Pettit led the Hawks to the division championship and, ultimately, to their finest hour. They beat the Celtics for the world championship, and Pettit scored 50 points in the final game, including 19 of his team's last 20 points in the 110–109 victory.

Bob Pettit retired from professional basketball after the 1964–1965 season. But before he retired he established several notable records. On February 8, 1964, he scored his 19,204th point to break the all-time NBA career scoring record. On November 13, 1964, he became the first player in the game to score more than 20,000 points.

At the time he retired, Pettit had scored more points than any other player in the game, although he ranked ninth on the list of most NBA games played. He was named Rookie of the Year in 1954, had made the all-star team in each of his eleven seasons in the league, was selected MVP of the all-star game four times and MVP of the league twice, won two league scoring championships, scored more points in the play-offs than any other player, had the most field goals scored by any NBA player and the second highest number of free throws and rebounds in league history.

Bob Pettit took with him into retirement 20,880 points and a 26.4 point average in regular season games, and 2,240 points and a 25.5 average in play-off games. He also took with him the undying gratitude of his boss, Hawk owner Ben Kerner, who knew that without Bob Pettit professional basketball would never have made it in St. Louis.

There have been players who possessed more natural ability than Bob Pettit. There have been taller players and stronger players, players who jumped higher, shot better and ran faster. But nobody worked harder, nobody practiced more, nobody tried harder to excel and, when it was over, he was considered by many to be the perfect player technically.

It was not always that way. It was not something that was innate. Bob Pettit was not born a great basketball player. He made himself a great player.

In his book *The Drive Within Me*, Bob Pettit said it all. He set down his personal philosophy, the reasons he

worked so hard and how it all started. How he went from
an unwanted high school player to an all-time All-Star in
the NBA. "The one thing my lack of ability did not break
was my spirit," he said. "In fact, it made me more determined to play. If you are bad, you could say, 'what the
heck, why should I embarrass myself? I'll never get any
better.' It's so easy to quit. I am happy I didn't."

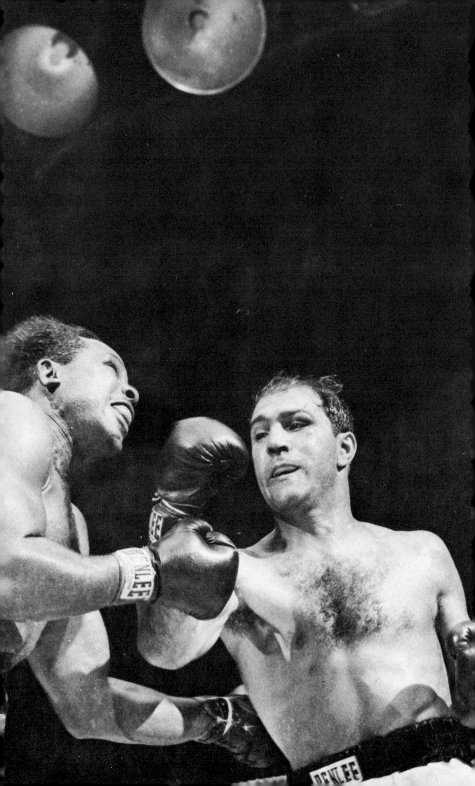

ROCKY MARCIANO

"He didn't even know how to face the punching bag."

The crowd at Madison Square Garden was on its feet, more than 9,000 voices hysterically yelling as one as fight crowds do when they sense the finish. They urged Rocky Marciano to put his man away, and Rocky responded as if on order. He slammed a left to the body and followed with a short right that bounced off the side of Carmine Vingo's face, and Vingo fought back with a strong right to Marciano's head.

For five rounds it had been like this. Twice Marciano had put his man on the floor, and both times Vingo had gotten up to stagger Marciano. The crowd loved it. They cheered and whistled and stamped their feet in approval, eagerly anticipating what they knew was inevitable. This was a fight that could only end with someone on the floor, the referee counting to ten over him.

Here were two outstanding heavyweight prospects, and it seemed a shame that one of them had to lose, had to be sacrificed. Carmine Vingo was a New York City favorite, a hard hitter from the Bronx who had lost only one fight in 17 and had scored 14 knockouts. Rocky Marciano was down from Brockton, Massachusetts. Another puncher. He was unbeaten in 24 fights with 22 knockouts, 9 of them in the first round. A victory over Vingo, especially a convincing one, would put him in the big time.

Marciano shook off the hard right and moved in recklessly, his short arms held high and close to his head. Vingo jabbed a left and started to fire his right, but before he could let it go Marciano whistled a short left hook to the head. Vingo went down in a crumpled heap, and the roar from the crowd was deafening.

Marciano turned and walked to his corner. With his back to his fallen opponent, he could hear the timekeeper's count coming over the loudspeaker . . . one . . . two . . . three. . . . Rocky reached his corner and turned to wait for the mandatory eight count, but there would be no eight count. Referee Harry Ebbets had signalled an end to the fight as he reached over to remove the mouthpiece from Vingo's mouth.

Rocky Marciano had won his toughest and biggest fight. He triumphantly threw his arms into the air and then embraced his seconds; he could hear the crowd chanting his name as he jumped around the ring. Then, as he turned to go to Vingo, what he saw made his heart sink.

Vingo was still not getting up. "Why isn't he getting up?" Rocky questioned. He saw Dr. Vincent Nardiello, the New York State Athletic Commission physician, bending over Vingo's body, and he saw Dr. Nardiello reach into his black bag, pull out a hypodermic needle and plunge it into Vingo's chest. A stretcher was brought into the ring and three men lifted Vingo onto the stretcher and carried him out of the ring. A wave of fear came over Rocky when he heard someone call for a priest. The crowd was hushed as Rocky's handlers grabbed him by the arm and half dragged him out of the ring.

In Marciano's dressing room, word came that Carmine Vingo was in St. Clare's Hospital, just two blocks from the Garden, in critical condition with a concussion and a possible blood clot on the brain. His chances of survival were slim. As quickly as he could, Rocky showered and dressed and rushed to the hospital.

Vingo was in a coma, Dr. Nardiello said, and his chances of pulling through were about 50–50. Rocky was visibly shaken. He paced the corridor nervously, and then he noticed a small, dark-haired, middle-aged woman sitting in a chair sobbing, her head in her hands. "Carmine's mother," someone said. Rocky went to her and spoke in

Italian. He tried to console her and tell her of the sorrow that was in his heart. The woman gazed up at him with a look of understanding in her face and forgiveness in her eyes.

Rocky waited until morning. Carmine's condition was still unchanged. Dr. Nardiello told him: "There's nothing you can do here. The best thing for you to do is to go home."

Rocky decided the doctor was right. There was nothing he could do. Speeding along the New England Turnpike heading for Brockton, Rocky sat in the front seat next to the driver, hardly saying a word. He was thinking of Carmine Vingo lying back there in that hospital, and he was thinking of the time he was two and became critically ill with pneumonia. He had heard the story many times.

Doctors had given him little chance of pulling through. His mother kept an around-the-clock vigil, ministering to her little Rocco, her first-born son, and praying to St. Anthony. After three days her prayers were answered. Rocco's fever broke and he grew up to be a strong, healthy boy.

Rocky's father, Perrino Marchegiano (the family's real name), had come to this country as a boy but had returned to Europe to fight for his new country in World War I. He suffered gas-poisoning and returned home a semi-invalid, able to work only part-time for the rest of his life. Money was scarce in the Marchegiano home, and at seven Rocky helped out with the family needs by earning money with a newspaper route.

As a teenager Rocky developed a consuming interest in sports and became an outstanding football center and baseball catcher. He left high school in his sophomore year to help earn money for his family, and he took a job with a landscape gardener. He held that job until he was drafted into the Army.

Boxing never held any great interest for Rocky when he was a boy. He preferred team sports, although occasionally he was forced to defend himself. The boys in his neighborhood were tough and played hard, and Rocky had little choice but to learn self-protection. Once he came home with a bloody nose, and his Uncle John installed a punching bag in the cellar of the Marchegiano home and began giving Rocco boxing lessons for self-defense. Rocco learned his lessons well. The better he learned, the less opportunity he had to demonstrate his ability with his fists.

By the time he was fifteen Rocky was a regular visitor to the Knights of Columbus gymnasium, where many amateur fighters and some professionals trained. Rocky was a hard 205 pounds, quite respected among his friends and somewhat impressed with himself. One day a professional middleweight needed a sparring partner and asked for volunteers. Rocky quickly accepted the challenge. Just as quickly, he realized he had taken on more than he could handle. The middleweight gave the cocky youngster a thorough going over, sending him home bruised and battered, determined never to put on a pair of boxing gloves again.

The promise did not last very long. In the Army Rocky had to make a choice between boxing and KP. It was not a very difficult decision to make. By joining the boxing team at Fort Devens, Massachusetts, Rocky found he would be allowed to miss KP and other tedious details.

After serving in Europe during World War II, Rocky was sent stateside to Fort Lewis, Washington, to finish his tour of duty. He entered the National AAU boxing championships in 1945 and made it all the way to the finals at Portland, Oregon, despite a broken knuckle on the middle finger of his left hand, incurred when he scored a knockout in the semi-final. It pained him terribly merely to clench his fist and, fighting with one hand, he was unable to make a contest of it. For three rounds he absorbed a thorough beating. Then, seconds before the end of the third round, he fired a wild right that landed flush on the jaw and his opponent went down. The referee could have counted to 100 and the guy still would not have climbed to his feet, but before he could reach 10 the bell rang, ending the fight.

Marchegiano had done very little punching in the first two rounds and, despite the last-ditch haymaker, he lost the fight and the AAU heavyweight championship to a fighter who had to be carried out of the ring.

Rocky figured he had fought his last fight. His career had ended before it started. The knuckle on his left forefinger was shoved high into his hand and the chances of correcting it seemed slim. But an Army surgeon performed an operation that saved Rocky Marchegiano's hand and his boxing career. Although his hand was in traction for two months, the operation fixed it as good as new. Rocky was ready for discharge from the hospital and the Army, but he decided to reenlist. He found a home in the Army. He was having fun boxing and the allotment checks were going home, so he had no reason to return to civilian life.

In the 1946 AAU championships he was again beaten in the finals. After that Marchegiano was transferred to

Massachusetts, where he met up with an old neighborhood friend, Allie Colombo, a master sergeant in the Air Corps. They talked over old times, and when Rocky told Allie about his boxing experience, Colombo was so impressed he suggested Rocky think about fighting for a living. "Okay," Rocky said. "You be my manager. Get me a fight and I'll turn pro."

Through friends Colombo arranged for Rocky to fight in Holyoke, Massachusetts, and on March 17, 1947, Rocky Marchegiano made his professional boxing debut as Rocky Mack against a fellow named Lee Epperson. He flattened Epperson in three rounds and collected $35.

After the fight, Rocky's left hand swelled and he was convinced his fighting days were over. He figured it would happen every time he punched with it. A few months later he was discharged from the Army and he went back to Brockton, making the rounds looking for jobs and doing a variety of work. He started on a construction gang for 90¢ an hour, but left that for a $1-an-hour job laying gas lines for the Brockton Gas Company.

It was Allie Colombo who convinced Rocky to take one more stab at boxing. Rocky was skeptical, but since he was bored and desperate he decided to give it one more try. Although he had had one professional fight, it was not under his own name, and figuring their secret was safe, Colombo suggested Rocky enter the 1948 Golden Gloves.

He won the New England heavyweight title and went to New York for the Eastern regionals, where he was matched with a boy named Coley Wallace, who was being hailed as the new Joe Louis. Wallace eliminated Marchegiano in a disputed decision which was booed by the crowd.

This convinced Rocky that he should continue fighting. Colombo and the fighter both agreed Rocky was ready to turn pro.

"First," Allie said, "I'm going to write to New York to get you a manager."

Through a friend Colombo got the name of "the best manager in the business," and on April 3, 1948, Allie Colombo sat down to write a letter to Al Weill, a New York character sometimes known as "The Vest." Weill had managed three world champions—featherweight Joey Archibald, lightweight Lou Ambers and welterweight Marty Servo. He had the skill and the connections to help Rocky go a long way. Weill turned the letter over to his trainer, Charley Goldman, who set a date for Colombo and his fighter to go to New York for a tryout.

Marchegiano and Colombo did not have carfare so they hitched a ride on a friend's vegetable truck, arriving in New York the day after their scheduled appointment with Goldman. They found him in the CYO gym on 17th Street.

Rocky and Al were a terrible sight when they walked into the gym. They were disheveled from the long ride and they smelled of onions from the truck. Charley Goldman was not particularly impressed with his new fighter. He was less impressed after Rocky climbed out of his street clothes and into boxing trunks. "He didn't even know how to face the punching bag," Goldman remembers. Nevertheless, he put Rocky into the ring to watch him spar with an experienced heavyweight. Rocky was awful.

Nobody ever started out in boxing with more things going against him than Rocco Marchegiano. For openers, he was going on 25 years old, which is about six years older than most fighters when they start their professional career. He had no defense and he could not even throw a jab properly. And he had unbelievably short arms—shorter than most middleweights—which meant he had to crowd his opponent to be able to reach him.

Still, Goldman saw something in the young man that interested him, and he recommended to Al Weill that he sign the boy to a contract. What Charley Goldman saw was the build of a fighter—strong chin, thick neck, powerful chest and well-developed arms and wrists. More important, he saw the intangibles that all great fighters have. He saw a hunger, a determination to succeed and a willingness to work hard. And work hard he did.

Charley Goldman is a gnome of a man, standing just five feet tall, but he is tough and demanding in the way of little men. He had been around fighters for almost fifty years, and what he didn't know about boxing had not been discovered. For three months he poured all the knowledge and experience of his fifty years into Rocky. And Rocky worked harder than he ever had in his life, until, finally, Weill told him he was ready for a fight. He had booked Rocky for a four-round fight in Providence, Rhode Island, against somebody named Harry Balzerian. Weill also told him he had a new name. By simply dropping the *heg* in Marchegiano, he came up with the new name—Rocky Marciano. Easier to spell, easier to pronounce, easier to remember and, besides, it sounded tougher.

The name Rocky Marciano was announced in the ring for the first time on July 12, 1948. Rocky kayoed Balzerian in the first round. He was brought back a week later in the

same club to fight a boy named John Edwards. He scored
another one-round knockout.

In the next three months he had seven more fights and
won them all, knocking out all but one of his opponents in
the first round. Now Rocky was moving. He had become
something of a celebrity in New England, and boxing people were beginning to talk of him as the outstanding young
heavyweight in the game. He had one more date left in his
rookie year—a four-rounder against a tough campaigner
named Gilley Ferron in Philadelphia on December 14.

In the first round Rocky connected with a left hook to
the jaw. As he did so, the pain shot right through to his
toes. It was a familiar feeling, and he knew he had broken
the finger again, just as he had in the Army. He finished
Ferron off with a right in the second, then reported to his
family physician to have the left hand put in splints again.

Marciano watched his dream flying out the window.
Everything he hoped for, everything he worked so hard for
seemed lost; he despaired of ever fighting again. But, for-
tunately, it was only a temporary setback. The hand responded to treatment, and by March 1949 he was ready to
fight again. He scored four quick knockouts in six weeks,
thereby convincing everyone, including himself, that his
hand was as strong as ever.

His kayo streak was stopped when Don Mogard managed to stay on his feet for ten rounds, but Rocky easily
won the decision. Goldman and Weill were pleased to see
him go the distance. Only one of his first sixteen fights had
gone beyond the third round, and it was important they find
out about his stamina.

After Mogard, Rocky scored three more kayos, then won a ten-round decision from Ted Lowry, followed by three more quick kayos. He had scored 23 knockouts in 25 fights and his reputation was growing. Boxing people were talking about the Brockton Blockbuster. But Rocky also had his critics, and they scoffed and said Marciano still had not fought anybody with ability . . . and it was true. By design, Al Weill was bringing Rocky along slowly to help build his confidence. Now the time had come to start moving him up.

For Marciano's last fight in 1949, Weill had selected a tough, hard-punching young heavyweight from the Bronx named Carmine (Bingo) Vingo. They were to meet in the first of three Madison Square Garden ten-rounders and it was to be Marciano's biggest test. Once and for all the public would find out about Rocky Marciano . . . and so would Al Weill.

It was the toughest fight of Rocky's young career, and for a time Weill felt he had made a terrible mistake. A left hook by Vingo in the fourth round was the hardest punch Rocky had ever felt. It staggered him and made his knees buckle, and it almost ended his sensational winning streak. But Marciano survived that punch and showed he could take a punch as well as give them. He fought back with a fury and an animal instinct that convinced the boxing world he was legitimate. He convinced them so strongly that now Carmine Vingo lay in St. Claire's hospital, a blood clot on his brain.

Now, making the long, painful trip back to Brockton, Rocky sat in the car, not talking, thinking only of that

poor boy lying near death. He should have rejoiced in his
victory, the biggest victory of his career. This is what he
had been hoping for, working for. This was the fight that
was going to put him in the big time, in the big money, but
he could not enjoy his success. Sadly he looked down at his
hands. They were the tools of his trade, like a carpenter's
awl or a plumber's wrench. Once he had been so proud of
his hands, their speed, their power. They had served him
well, taken him far, but he had never wanted them to put a
man in the hospital; to injure a man possibly for life, to kill.

He thought of the Army doctor who had fixed the
broken knuckle in his left hand, and he remembered how
grateful he had been to that doctor. But now he was no
longer grateful. Now he wished the doctor had never fixed
the broken hand. He wished he had not let Allie Colombo
talk him into becoming a fighter. It was no good if it ended
like this—it was not worth it if it meant a man's life. "If
anything happens to Carmine," he thought, "I'll hang up my
gloves forever. I'll never fight again. I'll never use these
hands to hit a man again."

His family and friends tried to convince Rocky that
what happened in New York was not his fault. It could not
be helped. But no amount of talking could console him. He
had put a man in a hospital, maybe killed him, and words
could not erase that from his mind. For two days he sat
around the house in a daze. He would not talk or eat, he
just sat. Finally, after two days there was good news. Carmine Vingo would live. He had come out of his coma. Dr.
Nardiello had stayed with him for 48 consecutive hours
and pulled him through.

For the first time since the fight Rocky relaxed a little. He felt as if someone had lifted a great weight from his shoulders. But he still could not put Carmine Vingo out of his mind completely, and he trembled at the thought of what might have been. Vingo was still in the hospital and permanent injury was still a possibility. Rocky knew he would not relax until Carmine was released with a clean bill of health. Marciano called the hospital every day to check on Carmine's condition, and he arranged to pay all the medical bills.

Madison Square Garden tried to get Rocky to return to its ring on January 27, but Rocky refused. He could not fight again until he was sure Carmine Vingo would be all right.

A week later a story hit the papers that helped Rocky's peace of mind. Edward P. F. Eagan, chairman of the New York State Athletic Commission, had begun the routine investigation which is customary whenever a fighter is seriously hurt in the ring. This time the investigation brought to light an interesting piece of information: When he was two, Vingo had fallen from a window in his home, suffering a fractured skull and leaving him with partial aphasia (loss of speech) and defective hearing. In 1947 he was warned to quit fighting because of the childhood accident, but he refused to heed the warning. "If I had known of his medical history," Dr. Nardiello said, "I never would have permitted him to fight."

This news absolved Marciano of guilt, for the slightest blow on the head might have injured Vingo seriously. Yet Rocky could not free himself of his feeling of guilt. Finally, on February 10, 1950, Vingo was released from the hospital. He would never fight again and he planned to go into business for himself; Rocky offered his help.

With Vingo completely recovered, Marciano was ready to go back into the ring. He accepted Madison Square Garden's offer to fight the main event on March 24. His opponent was to be Roland LaStarza, a highly rated heavyweight prospect from the Bronx. It was to be Rocky's toughest test.

Like Rocky, LaStarza was undefeated. He had scored 17 knockouts in 37 fights, but was known more as a boxer than a puncher. A part-time college student, Roland was a full-time student of boxing, a very clever young man in the ring who could make wild-swinging punchers look bad. And Rocky Marciano was a wild-swinging puncher who had relied almost entirely on power to get this far. He had not yet met a boxer of LaStarza's guile.

The fight was a good one. For three rounds, LaStarza did exactly as the experts predicted he would. He counter-punched and jabbed and boxed and he managed to stay away from Marciano's bombs, completely frustrating the New Englander.

To some it seemed that Marciano was outclassed, over-matched. Others felt he was rusty from a four-month layoff and still others asked other questions. Was he gun-shy? Was he still haunted by visions of Carmine Vingo being carried out of that very ring on a stretcher? Was he afraid to hit LaStarza?

In the fourth round Rocky answered all of those questions. He began to penetrate LaStarza's classic boxing form and land solidly to the body. Late in the round he smashed a right to Roland's jaw, sending him to the floor. Wobbly and obviously hurt, LaStarza got to his feet at the count of eight and, as he did, the bell sounded. In the fifth LaStarza abandoned his previous strategy and began slugging with his shorter, stronger opponent. They went at it until the final bell, the action never diminishing. They were still slugging away when the bell rang ending the fight, and 14,000 fans were on their feet cheering the action.

The decision was a close one. One judge scored it 5–4–1 for LaStarza. The other judge 5–4–1 for Marciano. The referee's card would be decisive: He scored it five rounds each, with nine points for Marciano and six for LaStarza. Rocky had won the toughest and most important fight of his life, and he was being touted as the next heavyweight champion of the world.

His opponents carefully selected, Marciano won his next nine fights, seven by knockouts and all in New England. He returned to Madison Square Garden to score a six-round knockout over Rex Layne, a highly rated young heavyweight puncher from Utah.

Now Rocky was ready for bigger and better things. He was sailing along precisely on the course mapped out for him by Al Weill. He was almost ready to challenge for the championship, but first Rocky needed a big name victim, someone who would be accepted by the public, someone who would help make Rocky believe in himself. Al Weill found just the man.

Joe Louis was old. Considered by many the greatest heavyweight champion of all time, he was 37 and should have quit years ago. His legs were tired and his reflexes had dulled. He was far from the Joe Louis of old, and the longer he continued to fight the more harm he did to the Joe Louis legend. Yet he stayed around because he needed the money and because he hungered for a return match with Ezzard Charles, who had taken Joe's title in a close decision just a year earlier.

This was the perfect fight for Marciano. Louis could not hurt him, and he had slowed enough so that he was an easy target for Rocky's bombs. Joe was slipping fast and Marciano was getting him at the right time. Joe Louis' name was still magic, and a victory over him would propel Marciano right to the top.

Still, Rocky could not help having mixed emotions about the fight. Just as any boy growing up in the late Thirties, Rocky idolized and admired Joe Louis, whose name stood for everything that was great and good in sports. He could remember sitting on the stoop outside his house on a hot June night in 1941 listening on the radio to Louis' fight with Billy Conn. He remembered the announcer's excitement because Conn was giving Joe a boxing lesson, and it had seemed certain the title would change hands. He remembered how it all turned in the thirteenth round when Joe caught up with Conn and knocked him out.

But that was ten years ago and now more than 17,000 fans invaded Madison Square Garden that October 26, 1951, to see two generations blend together like the sky meeting the land somewhere off on the horizon. They had come to see Joe Louis recapture the past or to see Rocky Marciano project the future. It was the classic battle of youth and age, the once great, fading champion against the ambitious and powerful rising youngster.

In the first round it seemed Joe Louis had found the secret of eternal youth. He beat Marciano to the punch and scored with a solid right to the head that made Rocky hold on to keep from going out right then. But Marciano came back in the second and third and pounded Louis with long, looping rights to the head. In the fourth and fifth Joe turned boxer, piling up points with his familiar, once-destructive jab. It seemed he had recovered all his old skills once again.

In the sixth Marciano opened fire with a volley of lefts and rights that made Joe Louis appear to turn old right there in the ring before your eyes. Once Joe feinted Marciano wide open, but he could not capitalize on the advantage. When he was young he would have shot home a thunderous right instinctively, instantaneously. But his reflexes had slowed, and although his mind knew what to do, his hands could not respond and Marciano quickly covered up.

Marciano had it all his way in the seventh, raking Louis with lefts and rights almost without retaliation. But as the round ended, as if to get in one more shot, Joe fired a left hook to the jaw at the bell that stunned Marciano and stopped him in his tracks.

It was all over in the eighth. Rocky caught Joe against the ropes and crashed a left hook to the jaw which sent Louis to the floor for an eight count. By some miracle Joe got to his feet and Marciano moved in for the kill. Eagerly he fired rights and lefts; then two suddenly swift left hooks sent Louis into the ropes, but he still would not go down. Marciano seemed to pause waiting for Joe to fall. And when he would not, almost reluctantly, Rocky crashed his strong right hand—dubbed his Susie Q—and Joe crumpled

through the ropes, his head draped over the end of the
ring and his feet dangling on the lower strand of the ropes.
Referee Ruby Goldstein signalled a halt to the fight, saving
Louis the added humiliation of being counted out.

"I couldn't help feeling sorry for Joe," Rocky said
later in his dressing room. "I saw him lying there, a great
fighter finished, and I remembered his greatness when I was
growing up. He was a hero of mine when I was young, just
like he was with other kids."

The old order of boxing changed that night. A new era
had begun. Joe Louis retired, stepping aside to make room
for the young.

Marciano's victory over Louis put him on top as planned but it had a side effect that had not been planned. He
was so impressive it was difficult getting opponents. He
waited four months for his next fight, and when he fought it
was a bad showing. He ripped Lee Savold to pieces, but he
failed to put him away. When the fight was stopped after the
sixth round, Marciano's reputation as a puncher was somewhat tarnished. Rocky said the long layoff was responsible,
and he insisted on fighting more frequently. Two months
later he knocked out Gino Buonvino in two and asked Al
Weill to get him Jersey Joe Walcott, the new champion,
who had recently defeated Ezzard Charles.

The press and public were asking the same thing, but
Walcott was not answering. He was too busy fighting an exhibition tour. He had waited a long time to win the title, and
he was going to make sure it paid off for him before he put
it on the line.

Meanwhile, Marciano knocked out Bernie Reynolds in
three rounds in May and did a slow burn when Walcott by-

passed him to put his title on the line against Ezzard Charles. Walcott won in fifteen rounds, removing the last ob-
stacle in Rocky's path for a title shot.

There was nobody left, but Walcott still refused to
fight Rocky, suggesting Marciano meet Harry (Kid)
Matthews, a light heavyweight from Seattle, to establish a
valid contender.

Marciano left no doubt as to his validity. He took his
vengeance out on Matthews, an overrated fighter whose performance could not match his reputation. Rocky belted him
out in the second round at Yankee Stadium. Now there was
no avoiding Marciano, and Walcott agreed to meet him on
September 23, 1952, in Philadelphia.

There were 40,379 in Municipal Stadium to see Joe
Walcott, the ageless, ancient cutie, dance and sidestep and
drop his hands and walk away from his younger, stronger,
harder hitting, cruder opponent. It was a perfect contrast in
styles—Marciano, a pursuer, was always moving in, moving
in, trying to reach his opponent with his short, powerful
arms; Walcott, skipping away, hitting and running, jabbing,
popping, retreating, leaving his opponent helplessly swinging at air.

This is what the fans expected and this is what Marciano expected. And because it was what they expected,
Walcott gave them something different. He dashed out of his
corner at the bell and fired lefts and rights in flurries almost
before Marciano could put up a defense. He pounded
Rocky's body, then switched to the head and whistled a left
hook to the jaw. Marciano was down for the first time in his
career, almost before he had thrown a punch. The crowd
was stunned with disbelief as Walcott walked away, fully ex-

pecting Marciano to stay on the floor. But Rocky did not. He bounded to his feet at the count of three and Walcott moved in to finish his man. He fired punches from all angles, but Marciano covered up, hanging on to get through the first round. He barely made it.

Hurt and humiliated, Marciano forgot all of his pre-fight instructions and went out after Old Joe in the second round. They plowed into each other viciously, staging rallies alternately, the trend of the fight shifting every few seconds but the momentum of the action never subsiding.

In the sixth they accidentally bumped heads and a cut opened over Marciano's eye. It bled profusely, the blood dripping in his eyes so that he was fighting through a fog. For three rounds, as Rocky bled, Walcott pounded a practically defenseless opponent.

Marciano's corner finally closed the cut by the ninth round and Rocky staged a rally that turned the fight his way for the next three rounds. But toward the end of the eleventh, Walcott staggered Marciano with a right to the heart, followed with another right that opened another gash over Rocky's right eye. Walcott was pounding him to the body when the bell sounded.

Jersey Joe Walcott continued his fury in the twelfth, and with three rounds remaining, he had built up a substantial lead. It was Marciano, not Walcott, who looked like the old, used-up fighter, and all Joe had to do was stay clear of Rocky's Susie Q for three more rounds to retain his championship.

The thirteenth round started and Walcott began dancing away, dropping his hands to his side and strutting in that familiar, cocky, irritating manner of his. Rocky shot a devastating left to the body that slammed Walcott into the ropes, and Marciano went after him, raging determinedly. Walcott tried to fight back. Something flashed through Rocky's mind. "I remembered studying the films of his fights," Rocky said later, "and we noticed that whenever he started to throw that left, he did a little step to the right."

Now, with Walcott backed into the ropes, Marciano anticipated the left and he waited, looking for the little step to the right. There it was . . . now! A feint of the head . . . a step to the right . . . and Rocky shot a terrible, bone-crushing right to the jaw. Joe's head snapped back and he dropped to the floor as if he had been shot.

Rocky rushed to a neutral corner, and he heard referee Charlie Daggart pick up the count . . . four. . . . Marciano looked at Walcott, lying there unmoving, and he wondered if he would get up . . . five. . . . The crowd was roaring, their voices building up a crescendo . . . six. . . .

Walcott rolled over and reached for the lower strand of the ropes . . . seven. . . . Now the crowd's roar was deafening, sensing that Walcott would not get up . . . eight. . . . Joe tried to pull himself up, but he slipped back to the canvas . . . nine. . . .

"He won't make it," Rocky thought, "he won't make it." The crowd roared and people were climbing out of their seats, pouring through the ropes into the ring, hugging him, pounding his back, lifting him. The ring was a mass of humanity that came to him yelling, shouting, cheering. . . . He was the heavyweight champion of the world and they wanted to be near him, to touch him.

He noticed a young, dark-haired, burly fellow in the crowd at ringside. Marciano called to him and the man

Rocky's long road to success culminated when he knocked out Jersey Joe Walcott for the heavyweight championship.

came into the ring, and Rocky threw a weary arm around Carmine Vingo's neck.

And miles away in Brockton, Massachusetts, the news came over the radio as a short, stout, dark-haired woman sat in a chair saying her rosary. She thought of another time when she sat saying her rosary as her little two-year-old son lay near death with pneumonia. She thought of how he had recovered and how, at the age of seven, he would awaken early each morning to deliver papers because they were poor and they needed the few pennies he earned on his paper route.

She remembered how he suffered with pain when he broke his hand, and how he worried that he would never be able to fight again. And she remembered how concerned he had been when he put that poor boy in the hospital.

She never wanted him to be a fighter. She worried all the time when he was fighting until he called her to tell her he was all right, he was not hurt. But this is what he wanted, to be a fighter, and now she remembered all these things about her boy and here he was, champion of the world and tears of joy streamed down Mrs. Lena Marchegiano's cheeks.

ROGER CROZIER

"It takes a special brand of courage."

In the first game he ever played in the National Hockey League, Roger Crozier made a terrible mistake. He forgot to duck. It happened in Toronto on November 28, 1963, the night Sid Abel, coach of the Detroit Red Wings, gave Crozier his first big chance.

"You play in goal in place of Sawchuk tonight," Abel had said, and Crozier, not yet 22 years old and less than a year out of the American Hockey League, gulped and said he was ready.

The next thing Crozier knew, big Frank Mahovlich, all 6'1" and 200 pounds of him, was bearing down to Roger's right, carrying the puck expertly on his stick and charging toward the Red Wings' goalie like a runaway stallion. Crozier crouched, tensed his muscles and waited for the hard, straight shot to come. He tried to anticipate Mahovlich's move, but Mahovlich was only a few yards away. He paused ever so slightly to brace and fire the shot, putting the full force of his powerful shoulders into it. The puck was a blurred streak, partially concealed by Mahovlich's body, as it whistled across the ice, starting low and rising slowly.

Crozier raised his right hand, attempting to catch the flying puck in the goalie's mitt that resembles a first baseman's glove. But the puck took off and sailed over the glove, smashing Crozier's face with a sickening thud and then bounding away. Crozier slumped to the ice, sprawling in front of the net. The side of his face felt like someone had struck a mighty blow with the full force of a sledge hammer. His teammates flocked around him and coach Abel asked Roger how he felt. Crozier insisted that he be permitted to continue in the game. He did.

The game ended in a 1–1 tie which should have been a cause for jubilation, but Crozier could not rejoice because of the terrible, painful, throbbing ache on the side of his face. He was sent to a hospital where X rays were taken. Roger Crozier had a broken cheekbone, a special cherished memento of his National Hockey League debut. He would be unable to play, the doctors said, for six months.

Two weeks later Roger Crozier was back in a Red Wing uniform. A week after that he was in the Detroit nets. Coach Abel had devised a special plastic mask to protect Roger's cheek. Most of the goalies were wearing masks, but Crozier had tried one and discarded it, saying simply: "It's no good. There are too many blind spots." So Roger Crozier had gone out to face flying hard-rubber hockey pucks with bare-faced courage.

It takes a special brand of courage merely to play in the National Hockey League. It takes a little bit more than that to be a goalie and face flying pucks that come soaring at you anywhere up to 120 miles an hour, the measured velocity of the great Bobby Hull's feared slap shot. And it takes a particular ration of bravery if you are Roger Crozier and you stand five feet eight inches tall and weigh 155 pounds and the bruisers barreling down upon you, trying to beat you into the ground, weigh anywhere from 25 to 50 pounds more than you do.

A goalie is bombarded with 25 to 40 shots per game—some of which he can see—and he is expected to stop at least 90 percent of them in any way he can. He can fall on them, catch them, knock them away with his stick, kick them away with his skate or allow them to hit some part of his body, including his cheek bone. Roger Crozier does his job as well as any goalie in the league, and better than most. Sometimes he does his job so well it hurts.

Roger Allan Crozier was born on March 16, 1942, in Bracebridge, Ontario, Canada, that unique part of the universe where every boy at a very young age learns to skate, to handle a hockey puck with a stick and to walk— usually in that order. As a boy, Roger played intermediate hockey for the Bracebridge Bears, and it was soon apparent the youngster had the makings of a future NHL star. In Canada, this is the kind of thing upon which dreams are built. The Chicago Black Hawks also thought Roger was pretty good, and they recruited him for their junior farm team at St. Catherine's when he was sixteen.

Crozier played magnificently at St. Catherine's, leading the team into the junior championships. He was rewarded for his great play with a professional contract with Buffalo in the American Hockey League—and with a bleeding ulcer at the age of seventeen, indicative of the pressures and hazards a hockey goalie must face.

He spent three years in the farm system of the Black Hawks, improving rapidly but blocked from advancement to the big team by Glenn Hall and Denis De Jordy, Chicago's great one-two goaltending punch. He was also stymied by the consensus of opinion that he was too small to take the rigors of goaltending in the National Hockey League. Coach Abel of Detroit had seen Crozier play for St. Catherine's and shared the skepticism of Crozier's ability to make it in the big leagues because of his size. But the scouting reports on him had been favorable, and Abel became persuaded to try to obtain the youngster.

Detroit was determined to dispose of tempestuous Howie Young, long known as the "bad boy of hockey," and Chicago had expressed an interest in taking a chance on him. In return, the Black Hawks offered defenseman Ron Ingram. Abel said he would take Ingram for Young if Chicago would toss in somebody he could use as a back up goalie behind veteran Terry Sawchuk. Somebody say like . . . well, this kid Crozier playing at St. Louis.

Chicago agreed and the deal was made on June 5, 1963. It was, according to Abel, the "steal of the century."

Crozier started the 1963–1964 season with the Pittsburgh Hornets in the American Hockey League, where he was to sharpen his skills and await the call from the big club. In just half a season at Pittsburgh, Crozier became the top goalie in the league and was named AHL Rookie of the Year. The call came from Detroit late in the season.

He got into fifteen games and so convinced Abel he could do the job that the Wings permitted Sawchuk to be drafted by the Toronto Maple Leafs. Crozier would be the Red Wings' regular goaltender in the 1964–1965 season.

It was tremendous pressure to heap upon a 22 year old, asking him to replace one of the greatest goalies in the history of the game. Sawchuk had just completed his fourteenth year in the NHL, the last seven with the Red Wings. He had started with Detroit, been traded to Boston and reacquired, and he was something of a favorite son in Detroit. The jury figured to be particularly critical of his young replacement.

"I was surprised to hear about Sawchuk," Roger said. "I didn't know they'd think I was ready to go all the way."

Ready or not, Abel threw Crozier to the NHL wolves and the youngster responded brilliantly. Early in the season he shut out New York, held Montreal to a 1–1 tie and turned in back-to-back shutouts against the Boston Bruins. Detroit fans completely accepted the newcomer.

But in a game early in December, the Toronto Maple Leafs swarmed all over him, peppering him with shots and humiliating the Red Wings' rookie goalie with a 10–2 beating. It was a harrowing experience, the kind that can shake a youngster's confidence and test his courage. But Crozier rebounded the very next night and showed the stuff he is made of by beating the powerful Canadiens, 4–1.

Crozier still had a long way to go. He still had a lot to learn, and by mid-season he found himself fighting the worst slump of his career. When the Wings lost back-to-back games to Chicago, 7–4 and 3–2, and dropped to fourth place, Abel decided it was time to make a change. Always edgy and jumpy, Crozier's nerves appeared almost completely shattered, his confidence destroyed. Abel became desperate as he wracked his brain to find a way to shake the team out of the slump. Invariably he came back to Crozier. Finally he had an idea.

"I've always been more concerned with a goalie than with anyone else on the team," Sid explained. "He's a very instrumental man. When he goes bad a whole team goes bad, and we were going very bad. The whole team wasn't playing well, and I figured if I could straighten Roger out, the rest of the team would pick up. In Roger's case, he has to have a breather once in awhile because of his physique."

Roger's physique had that "help-send-this-boy-to-camp" look, and that is exactly what Sid had in mind. Roger had not missed a game all year, and Sid felt it would be a good idea to give him a rest, send him away for a couple of days to forget all about hockey. On January 11 Abel put in a call to the Crozier house.

"Roger," Sid said when Crozier answered the telephone, "how would you like to go to Florida with your wife for a few days?"

"Sure, Sid," Roger replied, perplexed, "but I can't afford it."

"The whole thing is on us," Abel added. "You leave tonight, all the arrangements have been made. You'll stay three days and be back just in time for our game against Toronto. I want you to get a good rest."

Naturally, Roger jumped at the opportunity. There was a four-day break in the schedule for Detroit. He could go to Florida and come back just in time to catch the team plane to Toronto and not miss a game. Roger and his wife Arlene began packing the moment Abel hung up the telephone.

For three days Crozier did nothing but bask in the warm Miami Beach sun. He ate heartily, went to bed early at night and woke up late in the morning. He relaxed. Hockey was the farthest thing from his mind. In 70-degree weather he found it difficult to even think about ice. When the three days had ended, it seemed Crozier had been dipped in Ponce de León's Fountain of Youth. He felt like a new man . . . and the Red Wings played like a new team.

With their well-rested, sun-tanned goalie playing his best hockey of the season, the Red Wings went on a streak that pushed them slowly but steadily to the top of the standings. His first day back from vacation, Crozier beat Toronto, 4–2, and started a streak in which the Red Wings won seven of nine games. During that span Roger had one shutout and four times held the opposition to one goal.

The three-day vacation cost the Detroit management $500, but it was money well spent. The short rest proved to be just what Crozier needed. His play in the second half of the season picked up miraculously as he led the Red Wings to their first league championship in eight years.

Crozier played in every game in his rookie year, allowed just 2.42 goals per game, led the league with six shutouts and was awarded the Calder Memorial Trophy as the Rookie of the Year in the National Hockey League.

Satisfied with his first full year in the big leagues, Crozier went home to Canada to relax and rest up for the 1965–1966 season. He almost did not make it.

Early one August morning he was awakened by severe cramps in his stomach and was rushed to the nearest hospital. At first it was suspected his bleeding ulcers were acting up again, but doctors soon dispelled that theory. They pondered and probed to find the mysterious ailment. X rays showed nothing, and test after test brought them no closer to a diagnosis. For seven days Roger had to be fed intravenously, the only way he could get nourishment. And for seven days he remained on the critical list, given little more than a 50–50 chance of pulling through.

Eventually the ailment was diagnosed as a pancreas disorder known as pancreatitis. Ironically, it is something usually found in overweight people and, looking at Roger, it was easy to see why the doctors remained stumped for so long a time.

Three weeks after he was released from the hospital, Roger was in the Detroit training camp raring to go. The Red Wings were cautious. They refused to allow him to play until he had gone to another hospital for a complete checkup and had received a clean bill of health to their satisfaction. The doctors pronounced him fit for competition, but they placed him on a rigid diet. Nervousness and tension had always made it impossible for Roger to eat before and after every game. Now, with his new diet, even if he could eat it would not be much fun. He was forbidden fats, greasy foods, fried foods, oil, butter, salad dressing, spices, ice cream, soup, sandwiches and alcoholic beverages. Roger always liked a beer after a game; now he had to guzzle a thick, milky substance called Suspension Maalox, like a vanilla milkshake in appearance but not in taste.

Once, after shutting out Toronto, 3–0, Crozier went home to a wild celebration. He sat down at the kitchen table with his wife and ravenously downed ten glasses of water. Later in the season, Roger strayed from his diet and paid the penalty with stomach cramps. "I ate a hot dog," he explained, "and it bit me in the stomach." A man soon learns to live with his personal problems, and Roger learned to live with his to the point where it would not interfere with his job.

If the 1965–1966 season was not as good for Roger as his rookie year had been, it was not entirely his fault . . .

neither was it the fault of his pancreas. Crozier was the victim of a common malady known as "no support." The Red Wings' defense collapsed and Crozier found himself standing there, practically helpless, as opponents came pouring through almost unmolested to rain shots on the overmatched goalie. Crozier could not do it alone, and the Red Wings fell to fourth place.

Still, Crozier had a very good year. He was the league's iron man in goal for the second consecutive season, playing in more games than any other goalie (66) and leading the league in shutouts for the second straight year with seven. He played more minutes than any other goalie except Chicago's Glenn Hall, and although his goals-against average jumped to 2.78 per game, he and the ageless wonder, Gordie Howe, practically hauled the team single-handedly into the Stanley Cup play-offs.

If Crozier's goaltending during the regular season was merely outstanding, it was simply superb in the play-offs. Nobody gave the Wings a chance when they squared off against the high-scoring Chicago Black Hawks in Chicago in the opening series. The Black Hawks were tough to beat, particularly on their home ice. The Wings had been able to beat them just once in fourteen regular season games, and Bobby Hull, Stan Mikita and company had beaten Crozier for 51 goals. The year before, the Hawks had knocked the champion Red Wings out of the play-offs in the opening series, four games to three.

Crozier played well in the first game, but the Black Hawks won, 2–1, and Chicago fans were predicting a four-game sweep. Perhaps the Hawks were looking ahead to meeting the Montreal Canadiens in the final round, but the Red Wings slapped them down in the second game, 7–0. With the series tied at one game apiece, the two teams moved to Detroit where the Hawks scored another 2–1 victory. But Detroit came back to win the next three games, upsetting Chicago four games to two and moving into the finals of the play-offs against Montreal.

Crozier had been absolutely sensational in the Chicago series, holding the Black Hawks to ten goals in six games. Even the great Bobby Hull, who had scored a record 54 goals in regular season play, could manage to get into the Detroit nets just twice in six play-off games.

But Crozier was only beginning to warm up. Against the speedy-skating Canadiens, Roger was positively acrobatic. He was practically a one-man team, making saves from every conceivable angle and repeatedly turning back Montreal rushes. Time after time he stopped the dangerous one-on-one bursts of Jean Beliveau, considered to be the game's outstanding pressure player.

Incredibly, the Red Wings won the first two games of the series. And they did it on Montreal ice, much to the dismay of the strongly loyal and vocal Canadien fans. As the teams moved to Detroit with the Red Wings leading two games to none, the Detroit players were confident they could continue to confound the experts and romp off with their first Stanley Cup championship in eleven years. Not even a 4–2 Montreal victory in the third game could dampen the Red Wings' spirit or crush their hopes.

But in the fourth game Crozier had to leave the ice with a wrenched knee after 5:48 of the scoreless first period. The Canadiens went on to win the game, 2–1, and even the series at two games apiece.

Crozier returned for the fifth game. Playing valiantly on practically one leg, he was no match for the fierce Montreal attack. The fired-up Canadiens romped to a 5–1 victory. Now Montreal had the momentum, and although Crozier played brilliantly in the sixth game, forcing an overtime period after a 2–2 tie at the end of regulation time, Henri Richard pumped in the winning goal at 2:20 of the overtime period and the Montreal Canadiens were Stanley Cup champions.

Crozier's sensational play throughout the play-offs did not go overlooked, however. He was awarded the Conn Smythe Trophy as the Most Valuable Player in the tournament, and he received the $1,000 cash award that went with it. The Canadiens were miffed that the trophy should go to a player on the losing team, but the honor was a well-deserved one. Coach Sid Abel quickly came to the defense of his young goaltender. Sid knew, better than anyone else, what it took for Roger Crozier to become a star and what he had gone through the entire year.

"How in the world could they take it away from him?" Abel argued. "He stopped the Black Hawks in the semi-finals and he stood the Canadiens on their ears in their own pond. He stopped Hull on breakaways and he stopped Beliveau on breakaways. You can't possibly do more than Roger did for us."

It was a great tribute to Roger Crozier, who played the toughest position in the most demanding of all sports and proved that illness, injury and lack of size are no match for courage, desire and determination.

HERB SCORE

"Courage is not the exclusive property
of winners."

What a wonderful thing it was to be Herb Score in the
spring of 1957. He had not yet reached his 24th birthday
and he had played only two seasons in the major leagues,
but they were already dusting off a place for him in the
baseball Hall of Fame at Cooperstown, New York. Never
before had a young pitcher burst upon the major league

scene with such fanfare, such impact, such unanimous prediction for greatness. He had won 36 big league games and led his league in strikeouts in his first two seasons, something that had never before been achieved.

Herbert Jude Score was not exactly an unknown when word of the rookie left-hander with a mighty fast ball filtered out of the Cleveland Indians' training camp in the spring of 1955. In 1954 he had won 22 and lost 5 for Indianapolis and had struck out 330 batters, breaking a 48-year-old American Association record.

In other years, Score might not have had a chance at the Minor League record. The Indians would have had his left arm in Cleveland so fast, the rest of his body would have been two days behind. But 1954 was a record-setting year for the Indians, too. They won 111 games to breeze to the American League pennant, and pitching was hardly one of their vulnerable points.

During the spring of 1955 there was doubt that Score could move into the starting rotation, a quartet that consisted of Bob Lemon, Early Wynn, Mike Garcia and Bob Feller. But Herb not only broke into the rotation, he was the Indians' most effective pitcher in the second half of the season, prompting Bob Lemon to compose this little jingle: "There's no big four anymore. Score's got to stay in the store."

The rookie won the strikeout championship of the major leagues with 245 whiffs in 227 innings, and in so doing he broke a rookie strikeout record set in 1911 by the great Grover Cleveland Alexander. In all the years they had been playing the game, and with all the great pitchers who had come and gone, nobody who had pitched more than

200 innings had ever fanned more than one man an inning until Score came along in 1955. He was, of course, named the American League's Rookie of the Year at the age of 22. It seemed inevitable that Score would someday break Bob Feller's record of 18 strikeouts in a game and 348 in a season.

In a doubleheader against the Boston Red Sox on May 1, 1955, Feller pitched the first game and Score was scheduled to work the second. Feller won his game, 2–0, on a one-hitter to put the Indians in first place; he lost a chance to become the first pitcher to hurl four no-hitters when Boston catcher Sammy White singled in the eighth inning. It was a tough act for the rookie Score to follow, but he almost came up with a topper.

After three innings Herb had nine strikeouts. With six innings to get nine more K's, it appeared Score was going to break Feller's one-game mark. Feller listened to the game in the Cleveland clubhouse, and after seven innings Score had fourteen strikeouts. But he could get only one more in each of the last two innings and finished with "only" sixteen. It was a remarkable achievement for a rookie, even if it did fall short of the record. "I had to do something," Herb told the press, "after all, Bob had just pitched a one-hitter."

How good was Herb Score? In recent years it has become necessary to use Sandy Koufax as the yardstick against which all modern pitchers are measured. Comparison of the two left-handers is interesting.

By the time he was 23, Score was in his second big league season. He won 20 and lost 9 that year, had an earned run average of 2.53 and again led the major leagues in strikeouts with 263 in 249 innings. In 1959, at the age of 23½, Koufax was in his fifth season and still had not attained stardom. He was 8 and 6 with a 4.06 ERA and 173 whiffs in 153 innings. It was not until he had passed his 25th birthday that Sandy reached the 200 strikeout mark, with a league-leading 269 in 256 innings and an 18-13 record.

How good was Herb Score? In the spring of 1957, when he was the talk of the baseball world and Mickey Mantle was calling him the toughest pitcher he ever hit against, the Red Sox offered to buy him for $1 million. A publicity stunt? If that's what people thought, said Boston general manager Joe Cronin, let the Indians call his bluff. The ink on the check would be dry before you could say "Tom Yawkey is out of his mind."

There was nothing subtle, nothing deceptive about Score in those days of his youth. He would simply draw his left arm back and fire the ball in the general direction of home plate.

"You can tell a pitcher is throwing hard," says veteran umpire Larry Napp, "if there are a lot of foul balls hit against him. Usually we use forty balls in a game. When Score pitched we always had to have an extra dozen."

"Howitzer Herb" they dubbed him, the fastest thing since aspirin, which is exactly how big the baseball looked to hitters when Herb was pitching. Not even his lack of control seemed able to deter him from becoming one of the greatest pitchers of all time. What could, however, was a penchant for injury and illness.

From the time he was three and his legs were crushed by a bakery truck, until he suffered a spastic colon (a stomach disorder) in 1956, Herb was in the hospital almost as much as he was on the pitcher's mound. As a boy he suffered from rheumatic fever, a broken ankle and acute appendicitis. After turning to baseball, he was sidelined at various times with a dislocated collarbone, pneumonia and a virus; in addition, the rheumatic fever had left him with high blood pressure.

But Herb was a perfect hero. Tall, blonde and handsome, he had the look of the all-American boy. He was kind, courteous, unassuming, cooperative, intelligent, sincere and devoutly religious. And his name made him the delight of headline writers all over the country. INDIANS KNOW THE SCORE, they would write. Or, HERB SCORES FOR CLEVELAND. Also, INDIANS SCORE, YANKEES DON'T. It was beautiful.

Then came the night of May 7, 1957. The Indians were playing the New York Yankees in Cleveland's Municipal Stadium. Over 18,000 fans turned out to watch the awesome Score pitch against the fearsome Yankees, who had been demolishing pitchers and were riding a six-game winning streak.

In the first inning Score easily disposed of lead-off man Hank Bauer. Now he was working on Gil McDougald. The count went to 2 and 2. Score wound up, pulled back his left arm and threw his twelfth pitch of the game.

"I had to swing," McDougald recalls. "He had two strikes on me and I was surprised when he gave me a fast ball without much on it. I remember being surprised that he didn't follow through as he usually does. Perhaps that's why he wasn't ready to handle the ball."

The ball was a hard line drive, a white blur in the night. It hit Score in the face with a sickening thud. A gasp rose from the assembled fans, and then there was silence as Herb Score lay unmoving in a crumpled heap on the mound.

The silence was broken by the urgent plea of the public address announcer: "If there is a doctor in the stands would he please report to the playing field immediately." Within minutes, six doctors were on the pitcher's mound.

The ball had ricocheted to Al Smith, the third baseman, who picked it up and instinctively threw it to first. McDougald was out and, as he crossed first base, he turned and headed for the fallen pitcher. When he got there Score was already encircled by players from both teams. "He was such a mess," McDougald said, "I almost threw up."

Blood from his right eye gushed down the pitcher's face. Score, still conscious, just lay there, afraid to move. He could feel the pain and he could feel the warm trickle of blood oozing down his face.

"I thought about being blinded for life," Score said later. "I thought my teeth were knocked out and my nose was broken. I prayed to St. Jude. I was afraid to open my eyes, afraid I wouldn't be able to see. When I finally opened my eyes, it was like trying to see across the street in a fog."

A trainer wiped the blood away with a wet towel. Two players brought a stretcher and gently placed the pitcher on it and carried him off the field. "Now I know how Gene Fullmer must have felt when Ray Robinson hit him," Herb joked.

They carried him into the clubhouse and waited for an ambulance to take him to nearby Lakeside Hospital. When a reporter said, "I'll see you in the hospital, Herb," Score replied, "I hope I can see you."

After the game the Yankees dressed quietly. They had lost the game, 2–1, but their thoughts were not of the game. They thought of the injured pitcher and of their teammate, Gil McDougald, who was going through his own private torture. Some tried to comfort him, to reassure him that he

Catcher Jim Hegan was the first person to reach Score after McDougald's line drive sent him sprawling on the mound.

United Press International Photo

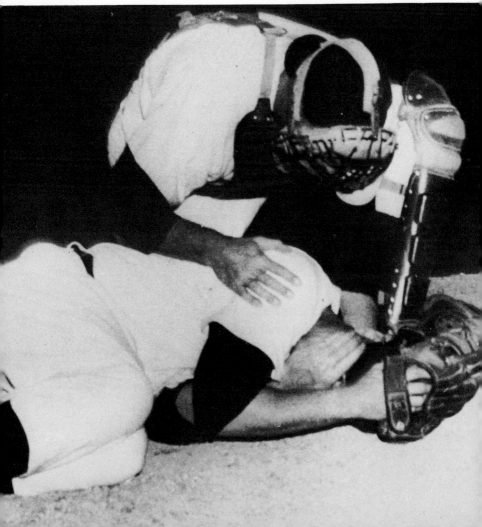

was not at fault. Others avoided him. What could they say at a time like this? Most of the Yankees left the clubhouse, but McDougald still sat there in his uniform as if in shock, talking quietly to Hank Bauer. Finally, he spoke in a loud voice, practically shouting, the emotion obvious in his face and his voice. "You hear me Bauer," he said, the words sounding like a solemn oath. "If he loses his sight I am going to quit this game. It's not that important when it comes to this."

In Lake Worth, Florida, Mrs. Anna Score heard the news of her son's accident. "I thought I would go to Cleveland," she told reporters, "but Herb doesn't want me to. What I would like to do now is see Gil McDougald. My heart aches for him. It wasn't his fault and I'm sure everything will be all right."

The following day three visitors went to Lakeside Hospital to see Score. They were Gil McDougald, Hank Bauer and Yogi Berra. But they were not allowed in to see Herb. The doctors warned there was still a 50–50 chance he would lose the sight of his right eye, and they prescribed rest, quiet and no movement. They told Herb about the visitors and he sent a message to the distraught Yankee.

"Tell Gil not to worry," he said. "Tell him it's not his fault."

For days Herb Score remained in total darkness, forbidden to move his head. Even the slightest jar could injure the retina beyond repair and leave him sightless in his right eye for life. Finally the crisis passed. His sight was saved, and three weeks later Herb was discharged from the hospital.

"I'll be in uniform and pitching by July," he vowed. True to his word, Herb joined the Indians on July 18. He threw a little on the sidelines and his fast ball was as swift as ever, but he had difficulty seeing the catcher's return throw. His depth perception was slightly affected. It would clear up in time, the doctors said, and when it did Herb would be able to resume his brilliant career.

He did not pitch in July. He did not pitch in August. On September 22 the Indians announced Score would take the rest of the season off to go home and rest up for 1958.

Once again they came in droves to the Cleveland training camp in Tucson, Arizona, in the spring of 1958. And once again the reason they came was to see Herb Score, the left-handed fireballer. But this time they came not to stand and stare in awe when Score fired his fast ball past hitters. This time they came out of curiosity and sympathy and in the hope of seeing this fine young man make a dramatic comeback.

For Score it was like starting all over as a rookie. He worked hard to make up for all the time he had lost and to erase the doubts that were in the minds of all baseball people. There were many things Herb had to prove . . . to them and to himself. How would the accident—and the layoff—affect his pitching? Would his fast ball still be as overpowering as before? Would his vision be impaired and, therefore, his control even more erratic than before? Most of all, would he be gun-shy on the mound?

The season opened and nothing Score had done in spring training erased the doubts, although Herb insisted he felt as good as ever and that he was pitching without fear. Catchers who caught him and hitters who batted against him in batting practice attested to the fact that his fast ball still had its smoke.

"I haven't pitched in almost a year," Herb pointed out. "It will take time for me to regain my rhythm, but I have no doubt I will." His optimism was not reflected in his pitching the first time he worked in relief.

Then, on April 23, he started against the Chicago White Sox and he was the Herb Score of old. He blanked the Sox, 3–0, on three hits and struck out thirteen. That was the convincer. It convinced Score and everyone else that he had found the touch again. Four days later rain cancelled his start, and on April 30 he pitched against the Washington Senators.

It was a cold, rainy night in Washington, D.C., and in the second inning Score broke off a curve ball and felt a twinge in his elbow. He pitched until the seventh and then could go no longer. He had pulled a tendon. Trying to come back too soon, he had aggravated the elbow, and from then on 1958 was another wasted season for the young pitcher who had broken in with such great promise. He pitched in only nine more games the rest of the year, finishing with a record of 2 and 3 and nothing but memories and hopes.

If the 1957 and 1958 seasons were filled with disappointment and failure for the young left-hander, the 1959 season was filled with frustration. He could throw without pain, but he seemed to have lost some of the zip on his pitches. Still, he was able to get by with guile and experience, and at mid-season he had a respectable 9 and 4 record.

Then things turned sour again. He pitched eight bad

games in succession, losing seven of them. When the season ended he had a discouraging 9 and 11 with a 4.70 ERA and 147 strikeouts in 161 innings, hardly matching his early promise. "I had spent practically two full seasons without pitching," Score explained. "All that time I was developing bad habits. When I tried to work I was favoring my elbow. If I threw low in a certain way I wouldn't strain my arm, but I lost my fluid motion and my rhythm and never recovered it."

Inevitably, people went back to the night of May 7, 1957, to explain the tragedy of Herb Score. He never recovered from the shot off Gil McDougald's bat, they said, and wasn't that too bad?

"I hate to have someone blame the eye accident for what I've done or haven't done as a pitcher," Herb said. "You're either a good pitcher or a bad one. I haven't been a good pitcher, but not because of the eye injury. I just haven't done the job. I don't feel put upon or that I have any particular cross to bear. I cannot offer any excuses."

Spring training of 1960 offered no greater hope. A day before the season opened, the Indians finally gave up on the young man who once had a $1 million price tag placed on him. They traded him to the Chicago White Sox, where he would be reunited with Al Lopez, his first major league manager.

Lopez had watched Score closely that spring, noticed he was throwing freely and felt he still had a chance to be a winner in the major leagues. If anybody could nurse Score back to form it was the patient, fatherly Lopez, a former catcher renowned for his handling of pitchers. Lopez had first seen Score in 1952 when the youngster, just out of high school, came to Chicago for a tryout. The manager was immediately impressed with Score as a pitcher and as a person.

Score was happy to be reunited with his former manager. He always liked Al and his approach to pitching. Lopez had helped build Herb's confidence in 1955 by putting him into the regular rotation even though Score was a rookie and the Indians were defending American League champions. Confidence was the one thing Herb needed again.

Lopez' first plan was to force feed Score. He put him right into the starting rotation with the hope that his faith in Herb would be transmitted to the pitcher. But Lopez' faith went unrewarded, and it was soon apparent he had overestimated Score's readiness. In six starts Herb failed to finish a game, and he went past the fourth inning only once. Twice he put twelve runners on base in less than four innings. He averaged $1\frac{1}{2}$ walks an inning and 14 a game, and had an earned run average of more than eight runs a game. This definitely would not do.

Lopez reevaluated his position and decided on a different approach. Score had hardly pitched at all during spring training because of an ear infection and he was not in shape for game activity. What he needed, Lopez decided, was work, work and more work. So the manager set up a rigid training schedule designed to get the pitcher in shape.

He pitched batting practice daily, and when he was finished he threw some more on the sidelines to strengthen his arm. He pitched at least two hours a day for almost a month and in a charity game with the Cubs, Lopez gave his student his first test. Herb passed, not with flying colors because it was only an exhibition game, but at least he passed. He held the Cubs scoreless for five innings. Now he was ready to try his arm out in a game that counted. He pitched two innings of relief against the Yankees, allowing three hits and three walks, but no runs.

Lopez noticed Herb was turning his head away from the plate after he delivered the ball, but he always did that. Even in his good days. He was always a poor fielder because of it. "That's why he was hit in the eye," Lopez said. "He heard the sound of the bat and he looked up and boom, a line drive hit him in the eye."

Lopez decided against trying to break Score of the bad and dangerous habit. He had been doing it for too many years, and to tamper with him now would make Score too conscious of the mannerism. If he had any chance at all of making a comeback, it would be ruined by making him aware of anything other than throwing as hard and as accurately as he could. A pitcher has enough to think about without adding to his burden.

Lopez ignored the flaw and reinstalled Score in the starting rotation. For six weeks it seemed he had performed the greatest miracle in the history of baseball. He might never again be the Herb Score of old, but he gave every indication of becoming an effective, useful, winning pitcher. And at 27 he still had a lot of good baseball years ahead of him.

In nine games from July 3 to August 20, Herb pitched eight or nine innings seven times. He had an ERA of less than two runs a game in that period, and although he won only three games, that was of little concern to Lopez because the Sox went into a hit famine and scored only six

runs in Score's starts. In one game against the Baltimore
Orioles, relying almost exclusively on his fast ball, he won
2–1 and did not walk a batter. Only once before—in the
minor leagues—had he ever pitched nine innings without
issuing a walk. If he was not as fast as before, he could
now compensate with better control.

Herb Score had made a gallant and remarkable comeback, and nobody was particularly distressed when he was
beaten by the Yankees late in August. For seven innings
he had set them down with just one hit—Bill Skowron's
home run. Then, in the eighth, the Yankees put two men on
base and Tony Kubek rapped him for a two-run double.
That was all for Score.

In his next two starts he could get only three outs, and
in the six games he pitched the rest of the year, he was able
to go seven innings only once. He was back where he
started, his decline even more mysterious than before. But
he continued to take the regression in his typical, philosophical manner. When people blamed the eye accident he
insisted it was not true. He took defeat gracefully, refusing
to accept any alibi.

There was life in the old arm for one last moment of
glory in 1961. The White Sox had lost seven straight games
when Herb took the mound on May 9 against the Cleveland
Indians. He won, 4–2, on a two-hitter. It was the last time
he would ever be the winning pitcher in a major league
game. Seventeen days later he was sent to San Diego in
the Pacific Coast League.

At San Diego Herb worked as hard as the youngest
rookie. He was determined to make it back to the majors.
He won seven and lost five and was recalled late in the

season. But he was practically a forgotten man the following spring, and on May 7, 1962, exactly five years to the day after Gil McDougald's line drive struck him in the eye, the White Sox announced they were sending him to Indianapolis, where he had started his professional career ten years earlier as a hard-throwing kid of nineteen with a ton of promise but not an ounce of luck.

"One of these days," Al Lopez said, "Herb is going to return to his old form and surprise a lot of people. Everybody's pulling for him. He's one of the nicest guys in the game."

So was Al Lopez one of the nicest guys in the game and it was a nice thing for him to say, but nobody believed him. Perhaps, not even Al Lopez.

At Indianapolis Herb was 10 and 7. He was worth another look in spring training in 1963, but nothing the White Sox saw was encouraging. The greatest heartbreak came when his mother died that spring. On April 7 the White Sox sent Herb back to Indianapolis. It was discouraging, embarrassing, humiliating, but Herb Score would not quit. He could not quit.

"If I quit now," he said, "I'll always have it on my mind that I might have made it back. I think I can still pitch and I'm young enough to come back. I've got to keep trying until nobody wants me anymore. Besides, I love this game too much to quit."

Herb never knew the meaning of the word. When he was a boy playing CYO ball on Long Island, he once showed up a half hour late for practice. His coach, Father Thomas Kelly, punished him for being late, and it was not until years later that Father Kelly learned the reason. Herb had left his spikes at home and he had to go get them after school. Because he had no money for the bus, he ran all the way home and back, a distance of five miles.

Years later, he was a guest at a high school football dinner. He listened patiently as he heard the coach say that although the team did not win many games, they had fun playing that season.

When it was his turn to speak, Herb was polite, but firm. "I don't see how you can have fun while you're losing," he said. "The object of the game is to win. I know someone has to lose, but how can you enjoy it? It kills me to lose. I'll tell you, honestly, I hunger to win."

Once, in the minor leagues, his manager Kerby Farrell went to the mound. He was going to tell Score, "Herb, you're not trying to pace yourself." Before he could get the last three words out, Score snapped, "Don't you ever tell me I'm not trying."

Nobody could ever accuse Herb Score of not trying, not even when he went down to the minor leagues for the third time. Not even when everybody was saying he had reached the end. He tried, but he fell apart completely at Indianapolis. He won none and lost six, completed only two games in eight starts and had an earned run average of 7.66. After the season the White Sox put his name on the draft list. The one-time million dollar baby could now be had by any other major league team for $25,000.

Nobody wanted him. It was over for Herb Score. His career was ended, but his story was not. Now he had to prepare for the biggest game of all . . . the game of life. He had a wife and three daughters to think about.

Courage is not the exclusive property of winners.

Courage does not always mean coming back from hardship and becoming a star. It takes courage to suffer one setback after another and to keep going . . . to refuse to quit. Herb Score never quit. He could have tossed in the towel many times and nobody would have blamed him or thought him a coward. He could have played it for sympathy. He could have talked of what might have been. He could have cursed the cruel fate that reduced him from a superstar to just another unsuccessful pitcher. But that is not Herb Score's way.

It takes courage to fight your way back from adversity. But perhaps it takes more courage when you are unable to fight your way back and you must forget the past and rebuild for the future. That is the kind of courage Herb Score possessed.

Not everyone can make the baseball Hall of Fame. Not everyone can be an all-America football player. Not everyone can be heavyweight champion of the world. Not everyone can win the United States Open. But everyone can try. Herb Score tried. The important thing is not to give up when things go wrong . . . to keep trying, keep working and never look back.

Herb Score did not make it back, but he did not stop trying. He did not stop trying even when he knew he would no longer be able to pitch major league baseball. He tried something else, and today he is a successful television announcer for the Cleveland Indians. He has no regrets.

"I have no regrets," he says, "because in my heart I know I didn't quit. I could have quit in 1963 instead of going to the minor leagues, and I'm glad I didn't. It would have haunted me the rest of my life. At least now I know.

I am convinced I went as far as I could go. I feel I am very fortunate to have played major league baseball; that God gave me the gifts to play in the big leagues. If I hadn't played I wouldn't have the job I have today. At least I'm still close to baseball, which is the thing I love best."

When he was a promising young pitcher with a blazing fast ball and a brilliant future, full of the confidence and hope of youth, Herb carried a poem around with him in his wallet. He still carries it. It is called "The Man in the Glass" and it best explains his philosophy in life:

When you get what you want in your struggle for self,
And the world makes you king for a day.
Just go to the mirror and look at yourself,
And see what that man has to say.

For it isn't your father or mother or wife,
Whose judgment upon you must pass.
The fellow whose verdict counts most in your life,
Is the one staring back from the glass.